TREASURES
ON THE
TIBETAN MIDDLE WAY

TREASURES ON THE TIBETAN MIDDLE WAY

BY

HERBERT V. GUENTHER

A newly revised edition of
"Tibetan Buddhism Without Mystification"

THE CLEAR LIGHT SERIES

Shambala Berkeley
1973

PUBLISHED IN THE CLEAR LIGHT SERIES BY:
SHAMBALA PUBLICATIONS, INC.
1409 FIFTH STREET, BERKELEY, CA. 94710

ISBN 0-87773-002-4

Originally published by E. J. Brill
under the title
TIBETAN BUDDHISM WITHOUT MYSTIFICATION

First Shambala Edition 1969
Second printing with index 1971
Third printing 1971
Fourth printing 1973

This book is published in the CLEAR LIGHT series dedicated to W Y Evans-Wentz. The series is under the joint editorship of Samuel Bercholz and Michael Fagan

MADE AND PRINTED IN THE NETHERLANDS

CONTENTS

PART ONE

THE BUDDHIST WAY

PART TWO

THE TIBETAN SOURCES

PREFACE

The title of this book, *Tibetan Buddhism Without Mystification*, came to my mind during one of the many discussions I had with His Holiness the Dalai Lama whose guest I was for the university summer vacations in 1961. He complained that much of that which purported to be information about Buddhism in Tibet was pure fancy and catered for the mystery-monger rather than for the earnest seeker of religious experience or the critical student of philosophy and that its rich symbolism, especially that of the Tantras, continued to be misrepresented grossly. He more or less pressed me to start writing about Buddhism as an inner experience which is of vital importance to our spiritual growth and development. In order to give an all-round picture of Buddhism as such a living power I chose four small texts that had been written by the tutor of the Eighth Dalai Lama. As the reader will find out these texts are a mine of information. They reveal clearly the inner nature of Buddhism as a path of development and they elucidate the relation between the Sūtras and Tantras and thus are invaluable in removing the many misconceptions about the latter texts. In the translation I have tried to emphasize the value of mystic experience, not only because it is the keynote of Mahāyāna Buddhism but also because it 'involves' man in actually following his path. At the same time I have attempted to show how its distorted presentation, its mystification, can be avoided. In this attempt I have studiously refrained from etymologizing (because we do not understand a word or a proposition by its etymology) and from rediscovering neo-Hegelian trends in Buddhism (although this seems to be the standard procedure by many Easterners and Westerners). This has necessitated a revision of almost all key terms in Buddhist texts and the introduction of new renderings. Against the likely objection to this innovation I can only say that stale, outworn and misleading terms do not help us in understanding the problem in question and that clarity, the prime concern of the scholar, demands that he distinguishes what can be distinguished by as clear and unambiguous labels as he possibly can.

The texts which are translated here for the first time, belong to the dGe-lugs-pa school of thought and in the notes to those passages which need further explanation for the Western reader, I have drawn copiously from other dGe-lugs-pa works. Although it would have been easy for me to quote from texts belonging to other schools of Buddhism in Tibet, I have refrained from doing so because I wanted to bring out the specific merits of the dGe-lugs-pa writers: the clear distinction between the various philosophical trends that were developed by the four major schools of thought in India and continued in Tibet; the preeminent interest in epistemological problems; and their traditionalism.

In the transliteration of Tibetan words I have adopted the system proposed by Turrell V. Wylie. It has the advantage of dispensing with diacritical marks. However, with personal names I have used a capital for the orthographic or phonetic initial, as the case may be.

I wish to express my deep gratitude to His Holiness the Dalai Lama, who lent me the texts translated here and who encouraged my work; Khri-byang bLo-bzang Ye-shes Rin-po-che, tutor to His Holiness, who was always ready to answer my questions and resolve any doubts concerning the meaning and use of technical terms; Geshe (*dge-bshes*) Ngag-dbang Nyi-ma of sGo-mang sgrva-tshang of Drepung ('Bras-spung) Monastery and the Mongolian Dalama Sog-po Ta-bla-ma rNam-rgyal rDo-rje, who both checked the presentation of Buddhist ideas by having me retranslate the whole English version into Tibetan and then pointing out preciser formulations. In particular I am grateful to the Mongolian Dalama for permitting me to reproduce the Tibetan texts which he had printed in India for the benefit of the Tibetan refugee Lamas.

I am also gratefully indebted to Prof. Dr. Jay R. McCullough of San José State College and Mrs. J. R. McCullough for valuable criticism and fruitful suggestions; Prof. Dr. J. W. deJong of the National University of Canberra for the lasting interest in my work and the help extended to me; Prof. Allen Atwell of Cornell University for the colour photographs of the Tibetan paintings in my private collection; Mr. Hans Dommasch, Medical Photographer at the University of Saskatchewan, for microfilming the texts; and, last not least, my wife Dr. Ilse Guenther who is, as always, the chief and patient sustainer of my efforts.

Saskatoon, Sask. H. V. G.
Canada

ACKNOWLEDGMENTS

I am grateful to the following publishers for permission to quote at some length from the designated works published by them, as follows: George Allen & Unwin Ltd.:

Louis Arnaud Reid, *Ways of Knowledge and Experience.*

Faber and Faber Ltd:

William S. Haas, *The Destiny of the Mind. East and West.*

The Macmillan Company:

F. S. C. Northrop, *The Meeting of East and West. An Inquiry concerning World Understanding.*

Routledge & Kegan Paul Ltd.:

C. D. Broad, *The Mind and its Place in Nature.*
C. D. Broad, *Religion, Philosophy, and Psychical Research.*
John Hospers, *Introduction to Philosophical Analysis.*

Charles Scribner's Sons:

William Ernest Hocking, *Types of Philosophy.*

LIST OF ABBREVIATIONS OF TIBETAN TEXTS QUOTED IN THE NOTES

Bdl	Byang-cub lam-gyi rim-pa'i dmar-khrid thams-cad mkhyen-par bgrod-pa'i bde-lam (commonly known as Byang-chub bde-lam)
Chz	The Collected Works of Yongs-rdzogs bstan-pa'i mnga'-bdag stag-phu yong-'dzin Ye-shes mtshan-can dpal bzang-po (Chu-bzang gsung-'bum)
GC	Grub-mtha'i rnam-bshad rang-gzhan grub-mtha' kun dang zab-don mchog-tu gsal-ba kun-bzang zhing-gi nyi-ma lung-rigs rgya-mtsho skye dgu'i re-ba kun skongs (Grub-mtha' chen-mo)
Khg	The Collected Works of mKhas-grub dge-legs bzang-po (Tashilhunpo edition)
KsNzh	gZhi'i sku-gsum-gyi rnam-bzhag rab-gsal sgron-me
Ktsh	Byang-chub lam-gyi rim-pa chung-ngu'i zin-bris blos-gsal rgya-mtsho'i 'jug-ngogs (Ke'u-tshang lam-rim)
Myl	Byang-chub lam-gyi rim-pa'i dmar-khrid thams-cad mkhyen-par bgrod-pa'i myur-lam (Byang-chub myur-lam)
Ngbl	The Collected Works of rJe-btsun bla-ma Ngag-dbang blo-bzang chos-ldan dpal bzang-po (lCang-skya ngag-chos gsung-'bum)
Phbkh	The Collected Works of rDo-rje-'chang Pha-bong-kha-pa dpal bzang-po (Pha-bong-kha-pa gsung-'bum)
SLNzh	Sa-lam-gyi rnam-bzhag theg-gsum melzes-rgyan
SLSHp	Sa-lam-gyi rnam-bzhag go-bde-ba'i ngang-gis bshad-pa
SngSLNzh	gSang-sngags rdo-rje-theg-pa'i sa-lam-gyi rnam-bzhag rin-po-che'i them-skas
Spl	The Collected Works of Thub-bstan yongs-rdzogs-kyi bdag-po rje-btsun Blo-bzang thugs-rje dpal bzang-po (sPang-gling gsung-'bum)
Tchks	dGon-gnas stag-lung brag-tu gsung-rgyun rgyal-ba'i bstan-srung-rnams-kyi gter cho-ga bskan-gso cha-lag dang bcas-pa dam-can dgyes-pa'i sbyin-phung
Tskhp	The Collected Works of Tsong-kha-pa (Tashilhunpo edition)
Zhdm	Byang-chub bde-lam-gyi khrid-dmigs skyong-tshul shin-tu gsal-bar bkod-pa dge-legs 'od-snang 'gyed-pa'i nyin-byed (Zhva-dmar lam-rim)
Zhl	Byang-chub lam-gyi rim-pa'i khrid-yig 'Jam-pa'i dbyangs-kyi zhal-lung

I.

THE BUDDHIST WAY

CHAPTER ONE

MAN-HIS UNIQUENESS AND OBLIGATION

Throughout its history Buddhism has claimed to be a path; and since it is the nature of a path to begin and to lead somewhere, its starting point and goal are of equal importance, although it is the goal that exerts a dynamic effect upon man's actions and in so doing directs his path or course of becoming. This goal is known by various names such as 'detachment from worldly and transworldly concerns', 'enlightenment', 'Nirvana', 'Buddhahood', and 'deliverance'. No doubt, these terms are ambiguous and what is to be understood by them may be considered from various angles. The goal may be seen on the one hand as something static and to be approached in a sense of possessiveness or, on the other, as a way of being which is active and dynamic. It is this difference in the goal-conception, the one static and the other dynamic, that marks the first great division in Buddhism: Hīnayāna and Mahāyāna.

It, further, would be a great error if we were to assume that apart from this distinction the goal is something uniform. There are considerable differences of opinion and expression concerning the nature of the goal, i.e., enlightenment, freedom, Buddhahood, in particular. In one instance deliverance means freedom from emotionally tainted responses which are felt to be the main cause for being tied to the world and for experiencing all kinds of hardships, disappointments and misery. In another case it is, in addition to the elimination of these emotional states and forces, an emancipation from the grosser forms of intellectual fog. Such a goal-conception is, more specifically, the recognition of the idealistic premise that things external to the observer do not exist apart from his experiencing them. Lastly, the goal is not only freedom from emotionally upsetting states but also from all forms of intellectual fog. In its most subtle form this is the belief that things really exist instead of recognizing that the notion of things, or a thing, is something defined by a set of propositions, and that to name is not to define them but is merely a way in which we assign and use meaning-terms. This difference in the goal-conception marks the second great division in Buddhism, that between Srāvakayāna, Pratyekabuddhayāna, and Bodhisattvayāna, the spiritual courses of (1) the pious listeners, (2) of the self-styled Buddhas, and (3) of those who pass beyond the turbulence of worldliness and a static trans-worldly quietude respectively. In philosophical terms Buddhism turns out to be a discipline that begins with a naive realism and passes through idealism to a point of view which is beyond determinate assumptions and qualifications.

This difference in the nature of the goal reflects on the starting point of the path, that is, the concrete human individual who travels the path in the light of his ideas about the goal to be attained which, on the one hand, tells him what he should be and, on the other, is nothing that he cannot be and become. The fact that the goal is not some vague abstraction which ultimately cannot mean anything, demands a new interpretation of the 'path'. The path is not a being-in-itself, something which connects two terms from which it is quite distinct, rather it is a going-to which pervades the whole of a complex manifold, from its foundation to its end. In other words, the path is a name for man's oriented becoming.

This pervasiveness brings us close to the concrete, man himself. But here we face the same problem as we did when discussing the goal. Man, too, may be viewed from various angles.

It has become customary to see man as a link in the chain of living things, one among many, and to concentrate on the question of his origin, which has resulted in a mass of far-fetched hypotheses with but few isolated facts. However absorbing these speculations may be they lead away from man and avoid facing the immediately present fact of his uniqueness which cannot be derived from something else and which is at the base of his humanity, in comparison to which every other form of life seems to be a degeneration from man. Buddhism recognizes six forms of life: denizens of hell, spirits, and animals as its negative features, and men, demons, and gods as its positive ones. Even if we are reluctant to accept such a conception of life, because apart from men and animals the other forms are not physically true, they are nevertheless psychologically so, and whether we still believe in heaven and hell, man himself remains the abiding centre of interest. It is man who at any moment may degenerate into unadulterated brutishness, create hells for himself and others, and lead a shadowy existence of spiritual starvation, or may over-reach himself into a state of godhood and the demoniac.

To concentrate on man in the concrete is therefore to see him in his body as he expresses himself through it. I deliberately avoid speaking of man's physical aspect in this connection, although the Buddhist texts seem to make the same distinction as we do when we speak of the physical and the mental. Such distinctions, valuable as they are for particular disciplines, more often than not blur the differences in conception which occur in various cultural settings. They tend to make us overlook the uniqueness of man, his humanity which is essentially of a psychological order because it is defined by references to certain kinds of mental processes, attitudes and actions prompted by them. Thought and action go together, although it is the latter that is more easily perceived as it occurs in a physical setting. Hence in order not to read our categories of the mental and physical into Buddhism and then rashly judge that after all everything is the same, it is better to refer to that which would look like the physical aspect as man's active aspect as it manifests itself in his being with others. In this way we focus not so much upon what man is as how he acts. At the same time we recognize his obligation to act as a human being. Of course, he may not fulfil his obligation because to do so would necessitate a thorough awareness of his being human and it is much easier to avoid such an awareness and its inherent responsibility by seeking to justify and cling to outworn schemes of values which are assumed to have been fixed once for all by divine sanction. But this is precisely to lose one's uniqueness, to miss one's chance of being human and to succumb to the dehumanizing forces of un-knowing. However, once the awareness of being man and of the obligation it entails is awakened, we find a value that is relevant to our concrete existence here and now. This value reinforces action and binds us to it. The intimate connection between fact and value and its relation to action in the framework of human existence is clearly stated by Tsong-kha-pa who, following an old tradition, demands that eighteen qualities and conditions must be fulfilled before man can be considered a human being. Of these eight relate to the uniqueness of his being man, while the remaining ten indicate the nature of his response to stimuli in connection with his spiritual growth and development [1]. Tsong-kha-pa's words are [2]:

"The eighteen qualities and conditions which constitute man's uniqueness and fortune must be complete, because those who live in evil forms of life are tormented by unbearable suffering and those who are among the

---

[1] These eighteen qualities have been explained in detail in note 1, p. 78 and note 3, p. 80.

[2] *Tskhp* II 2, 84a seq. As this passage is extremely concise and as a purely literal translation (a 'crib') would not convey the meaning, the latter has been supplied from *Zhdm* 33b-36b, which comments on Tsong-kha-pa's dissertation.

gods and in the realm of the blessed have little to be dissatisfied with. For this reason I must realize enlightenment at a time when I have the above eighteen qualities and conditions. The basis for winning enlightenment is the presence of these conditions which constitute my uniqueness and fortune. If I were to think that I could win this enlightenment when I find this unique occasion in another, future existence, I must think how hard it is to find it.

"The difficulty relates both to the effect and to the cause. As to the effect, i.e., my present unique occasion, I have to think of it in relation to the different kinds of living beings and of how difficult it is to find it among those who are similar to me. In the former case, the very body of a human being appears to be a sport in comparison to the multitude of animal forms, and in the latter even among men themselves, the presence of the eighteen qualities and conditions is something exceptional.

"As to the cause of my uniqueness I have to think of the difficulty in general and in particular. In the first case it means that in order to find a human body it is necessary to store powerful, wholesome Karma, and this is very rare. In the latter case, impeccable ethics and manners as the motivating power for winning enlightenment must be present as a solid foundation, liberality and other virtues as its companions, and proper resolutions as the connecting links. And these also are something very rare.

"If I were to think that, although this human life is difficult to win, it has been achieved and will last, I have to consider its transitoriness which involves three premises: the certainty of death, the uncertainty of the hour of death, and the danger of death coming any moment without delay."

With singular insight Tsong-kha-pa exposes the attitude of escape and evasion that underlies most of man's actions. Man is afraid to face the facts and prefers to think of Utopian schemes in which he will be relieved of responsibility. Tsong-kha-pa also formulates the inescapable facts and limits of our existence which, as a rule, man tries to dismiss from his considerations. He challenges the unqualified assumption that suffering achieves dignity and is a road to godhead. No doubt, suffering often acts as a powerful stimulus, but there is a limit to it. Once it passes beyond endurance it breaks man and dehumanizes him; and the infliction of suffering on others in the belief that it has a chastening effect, is an equally perverse notion. On the other hand, absence of suffering is no stimulus to action. If there is nothing to interfere with my comfort I have no incentive to act. Moreover, as Tsong-kha-pa points out [1], this leads to a degeneration of all cognitive functions. First, all one's senses become blunted and like a fool one is unable to use one's intelligence and to discriminate. Then, in abject stupidity, one is unable to see below the surface. Therefore man is superior to each form of life, hell and heaven, by virtue of that which is lacking in the one or the other, but which he possesses by himself.

Although man is in constant danger of becoming dehumanized and of being hemmed in by death, these forces need not shatter him. It is a fallacy to think that man has been cast into the world without rhyme and reason, and that his humanity is a random happening and a sad mischance, as some Continental existentialist thinkers hold. But it is equally abortive to attempt to explain away these forces and to imagine that he lives in a friendly universe and merges his finitude with the infinity of an absolute spirit in the manner of the idealists. Both ways commit violence to man's uniqueness. The existential limits clamour for an understanding and stir us to immediate action and thereby, so to speak, enable us to transcend them.

Therefore, the contemplation of death, which is insisted upon in the texts after they have stated man's uniqueness, is not some morbid preoccupation. This would be the case if it were an end in itself. This is not so, but it serves as a reminder that it will never do for man to postpone his decisions, that any hesitation to fulfil his obligation is to lose his humanity. At the same time this contemplation challenges our tendency to consider death as something universal which, because of its universality, we avoid considering as something that might concern us now. This is but another way to escape facing our humanity and the responsibilities that go with it. Facing this problem and being aware of our obligations, in short, moral integrity, is closely connected with the thought of death. Yet death does not point to the futility of life, but to its intrinsic importance and value. Man's active aspect on the basis of the Buddhist texts therefore can be summed up as follows:

1. Man must decide here and now;
2. Man's humanity is not a mischance but the outcome of his actions;
3. Man is under obligation to act in such a way that his humanity is preserved; and
4. This is only possible if he is reminded of his humanity at every moment. Any postponement therefore may be his undoing.

Closely related to this active side of man is the intentionality of all

---

[1] *Tskhp* IV 1, 14b.

his experiences. That is to say, in acting we are conscious of our actions as they proceed towards the goal. The end is always intentionally present before our minds and directs our actions. So also in planning and deliberating, in mapping out the course of our becoming, we are aware of the end in view and of the way to it. Here it will be important to distinguish between two kinds of knowledge and awareness which we will call the practical-theoretical and the mystic-intuitive one.

We are familar with the former and have developed it to the degree that it unites with our active tendencies. Much of that which many of us regard as guaranteed, as pure fact, is but the contribution of theory. Most of our concepts relate to a certain purpose or the thing intended, and even our sensations and feelings are full of craving and desire. This practical-theoretical awareness is engaged in ordering a world of things and artifacts. It is not concerned with things as they are in themselves, but only with them as they are for a purpose. It is obvious that the horizon of such an awareness is necessarily restricted and its points of view rather biased.

The second kind of awareness is grounded in the conviction that we can know the real nature of the world we live in without distortion. It holds that if reality is in any sense 'behind' the appearance, there is still nothing concealed from us. We may have a direct perception of reality as it is, and since reality must appear to us if we are to know it, its appearance is exactly as it is and not a mere shadow or semblance of something unknowable in itself. Thus there is a tremendous difference between the conception of the function of this mystic-intuitive awareness and the doctrine of the Unknowable. This direct knowledge of the real, which is claimed both by intuitionism and mysticism (which has nothing to do with mystification and the occult of the mystery-monger), is gained only after arduous practice, when detachment from all practical concerns and situations has been achieved and an unrestricted perspective been won. However, its attainment is of primary importance, because its insights give us more accurate and adequate knowledge of the thing in question than the practical awareness with its relation to a restricted purpose is ever able to do. In the last analysis even the development of practical awareness does not aim at the ownership or possession of things, rather it seeks an intentional union with them. Therefore to pursue this knowledge does not mean to realize one's oneness with the Absolute, since the Absolute is not known objectively but is the subject of the knower. Certainly such self-union does not involve any knowledge, because knowledge implies a known and a knower. The mystic-intuitive awareness, however, involves an object and always includes an aspect of duality which is transcended in what is called the noetic union. This means that the noetic act which is grounded in the knowing agent and exists as an indeterminate relational form is terminated by the object having its own ground, with which formal identity is achieved. The mystic-intuitive awareness is and remains relational in structure.

What these two types of knowledge give us is called the 'conventionally true' and the 'ultimately true' respectively. They never occur in isolation and, in a sense, are the beginning of the noetic enterprise of man. However unless fully developed their union is vague and confused. It is only by knowing the real through the mystic-intuitive knowledge that we can know the conventionally true which may enable us to act in a proper way. In other words, intuition and practical thought must go together. In Buddhism, unlike in Kantianism and certain trends in modern existentialism, the development of the mystic-intuitive knowledge is of primary importance and that of the practical awareness is subordinate to it. The development of the former has its effect on the latter, and it is in the area concerned with an understanding of that which is meant by the conventionally true that we meet with different interpretations according to the different philosophical trends in Buddhism.

There have been four great philosophical schools, all of which are still (or were) studied in Tibet. They are the Vaibhāṣikas representing a naive realism, the Sautrāntikas with a critical realism, the Vijñānavādins who are very similar to the idealistic-mentalistic thinkers in Western philosophy, and the Mādhyamikas. The latter divide into two groups, the Svātantrikas who still upheld the idea of an essence, and the Prāsangikas who instead advocated a philosophy which superficially looks like nominalism. The three latter trends have, each in its own way, been favoured by the four great Tibetan schools. The dGe-lugs-pas adopted the viewpoint of the Prāsangikas as did the early bKa'-brgyud-pas; the Sa-skya-pas favoured the Svātantrikas and on the whole became very eclectic; and the rNying-ma-pas attempted a harmonious unity of the Vijñānavāda and the Mādhyamika philosophies. According to this division, for the Prāsangikas to understand the conventionally true means to comprehend that the things we encounter do not exist apart from our giving them names in the manner which L. Wittgenstein would call the 'language game'. For the Svātantrikas it means that although things do not really exist, they have a sort of apparitional existence and quality; and for the Vijñānavādins it means that things do not exist as objects external to the observer but experientially-propositionally. Such a variety of conceptions cannot but have a strong effect on the way we deal with 'things', and naturally on the idea we have of ourselves.

This noetic enterprise, which aims at finding an unbiased point of view and therefore is essentially important for man's acting as a human being instead of floundering along among ideas about what might be, and so doing himself more harm than good, consists of three major steps. Tsong-kha-pa declares [1]:

"The noetic enterprise is subsumed under the topics of (1) detachment from practical concerns, (2) the development of an enlightened attitude, and (3) an unbiased outlook.

"That which is the positive factor for attaining deliverance and omniscience must be considered as constituting these three topics or as being supported by them. Although the two last are the motivating powers for winning omniscience, one speaks of three such powers by assigning them, too, a certain power. This is so because once detachment is in the process of being effected all the elements forming the causal situation of winning supreme enlightenment are forthwith understood. If there is no feeling of disgust, overpowering the addiction to the pleasures and riches of the world, there will be no active interest in deliverance, and hence detachment has to be practised; and if there is no concern for others, although there be detachment and an active interest in deliverance, it will not become the motivating power of winning enlightenment. Hence an enlightened attitude has to be developed. Although these two direct the mind towards omniscience and deliverance, they are unable to break the belief in an ego, and hence an unbiased outlook has to be won. But since there is no certainty about the mental level of individuals, there is also none about the order of these topics.

"In addition to this consideration of the reason for practising these three topics, detachment, first of all, consists in finding fault with the desire for self-assertion, since this is the root of all fancies. Then, in order to banish the desire for the world, one has to think of the misery of the world in general by taking into account two kinds, that of potential misery and that of change, and in particular that of misery itself; one has to feel that about which one thinks. Lastly, in order to apply oneself to good and avoid evil, one must consider the fact that happiness and sorrow derive from good and bad actions, and in direct experience one must understand the infallible relation between the cause and effect of one's actions. By practising this for a long time, one will feel disgusted

[1] *Ibid.*, II 2, 84b.

with the world in the sense that one wants to be separated from it; and once this feeling is present, detachment as the desire for deliverance comes by itself."

Two points have to be noted in particular. An 'enlightened attitude' is qualified as 'supreme'. This is to emphasize the Mahāyānist conception of enlightenment as an active and dynamic way of being, and not the static ideal of the Śrāvakas and Pratyekabuddhas who each have their own idea of what enlightenment may mean, namely the expulsion of all that obstructs integration and the attainment of all that furthers it. In a very restricted sense, to develop an enlightened attitude means to become and remain goal-conscious.

The other point to note is the rejection of any belief in an ego or self. The Tibetan term (*bdag-med*) is more comprehensive as it relates to any form of ontological ideas, be they in connection with a personal self or objects of nature. The rejection of an individual self or a Pure Ego is common to all the philosophical schools mentioned above, for whom, with the exception of the Prāsangikas, the belief in a Pure Ego is the coarse or crude form of the belief in a self, while the subtle one is belief in a self inseparably connected with a person as a sort of self-sufficient substance holding together the various constituents of an individual's body-mind. This subtle belief is for the Prāsangikas a coarse one, because they reject any ontological conception.

In order to achieve all this man needs 'spiritual friends', who are any persons from whom we can learn. It is important that we meet true friends who set us on a positive way so that we walk towards a positive goal that promises to help and benefit others. To follow spiritual friends presupposes a trust, which implies on the one hand that it is the Buddha who speaks through them and that the more we learn and understand the more we share their favours. To be favoured by Buddhas means to gain deeper understanding of reality. It is never an unmerited favour or grace. On the other hand, this trust is also a readiness and willingness to follow the advice of spiritual friends in a sort of thanksgiving for all that they have done and are still doing for us [1].

---

[1] So also in greater detail in *Bdl* 4b-5b; *Myl* 26b.

CHAPTER TWO

DIFFERENT TYPES OF MAN

The fact that man as a concrete individual has always been of primary importance in Buddhism, has prevented it from accepting the idea that all men are equal. This, though often insisted upon with much rhetoric, is obviously false not only where psychological aptitudes and talents are concerned but also where man's dealings with others are involved, particularly in the field of education and learning. If equality has any meaning it only can suggest that man should act humanely, and even here a gradation in conduct is conspicuous.

Buddhism has always favoured a triple classification which has been developed on the basis of knowledge born of the desire to cultivate and refine the personality and to achieve deliverance and spiritual freedom. It is true that the Buddhist classification seems at first glance to be of a rough and ready sort. Nevertheless its fundamental merit lies in the fact that it recognizes three main types as distinct, if not extreme, features of a continuous variable. It therefore takes into account the rich variability and uniqueness of the human personality. Each man has an inferior, mediocre or superior nature, and each subsequent development or change from an inferior to a higher nature is evolved in the course of systematic training. 'Three types of man' is thus a term emphasizing the variability of the human individual.

Not only are there differences in intellectual capacity, the learning process itself also is not entirely a matter of intelligence as narrowly defined, for it involves emotional and social qualities of all sorts. This is particularly so in matters having to do with our symbol systems. Since these are basic to personality, it is clear that self-involvement must enter into most of our important acts, not only in the sense that it is necessary to be aware of how others see us but also of how we view ourselves. No process of learning is possible without a self-image, without the idea of how we are going to be. The triple classification evolved in Buddhism has this double aspect. In its determination of superior, mediocre, and inferior natures it is concerned with how others see us, while regarding that which is done by each type it is concerned with how we view ourselves. Inasmuch as education and learning are graded processes, it will never do to skip any steps in them, unless one does not care whether the whole edifice that is going to be erected is shaky or not. It is here that the insistence of the Buddhists on their path being a graded course proves to be really sound. This path may be said to start with a few general principles and gradually, the further it goes, the more specialized it becomes until it finds its climax in what is commonly known as Tantrism. Even this latter aspect is a graded process open only to those whose intelligence and appreciation have been sharpened by the preceding courses. Therefore, if one pursues a self-determined concept of training, and if one thinks that it will be sufficient just to pick out some item or other which suits one's momentary whim or which tickles one's curiosity, it can result only in absurd statements which, probably because of the lack of the proper perspective of the whole context, are nevertheless held with authoritative fervour as valid. If a person were to practise religion on such haphazard information spiritual disaster would be bound to overtake him.

At the lowest level we find the man whose sole aim is to emphasize his own happiness. Although he may adopt a sort of 'fleeting-hour' plan, in the back of his mind he is motivated by hedonistic ideas and action patterns designed to ensure great and strong happiness for the major part of his life as opposed to long years of boredom and frustration. Since belief in the survival of the personality is common to most people, the above attitude lends itself admirably to the wish to pursue happiness after death. However, unlike most other survival theories Buddhism did not for a moment accept that survival entails the immortality of a soul. There is nothing everlasting and the fact that life continues does not prove that there must be some determinate factor which will continue unchanged.

This continual pleasure-hunting can be justified by two empirical facts: transitoriness through death and the misery of unhappy states. Transitoriness we can observe everywhere; in the change of seasons, in the fleeting hours of day and night, in the passing away of those who are dear to us... All this has an immediate effect on us. None of us can avoid death, which may strike at any moment.

The unhappy states, apart from that of animals, are symbolized by those who live in hell and the poor spirits. It is a fallacy to think that they are only unreal fantasies or, at best, aesthetic images. This may be so for those of us who have developed the faculty of first speaking with moral pathos about good and evil and then, when we ought to commit ourselves, avoiding the issues and leaping to the aesthetic, conjuring up pictures of illusory grandeur. But when and where the conception of hells and spirits is indigenous it serves to formulate existentially experienced reality. The perception of hells and spirits means an active relation, be this a struggle against or a surrender to them. Admittedly, to us, the language which speaks of hells and spirits is for the most part outmoded, if not even meaningless, and its challenge entirely passes us by. The main objection is that the description of hells and of the spirits speaks of the transcendent in terms of an external and objective world, in which it can never be expressed adequately. The knowledge of hells and spirits can be existential only, in terms of that which is done to us and of our responses and decisions. We do not now believe in hells and spirits and an objective revival is dangerous, but when we think deeply on matters of the spirit and of religion such expressions as 'to pass through hell' and 'to have seen a spirit' are not bad descriptions of ourselves and other people we know when in certain states. Certainly, hells and spirits are elements of a mythic language, and we do not want to keep dead story-pictures; but if they are symbols by which we can make the reality of religious experience more alive in ourselves, we cannot dispense with them. The language which refers to hells and spirits has an essentially material element in it, but its intention is not finally material. If it were so it would be mere idolatry, a sentimentality moving in aesthetic pictures. The Fifth Dalai Lama has succinctly stated the existential significance of the idea of hells and spirits [1]:

"The way of thinking which prevails nowadays consists in looking, as it were, at the misery of others from the viewpoint of an extroverted mind and in quoting a few scriptural texts; it is never a load on one's heart. For instance, when one sees the various preparations for the execution of a criminal in the king's court, it may happen that, pleased with the thought that justice is done, feelings of disgust and thoughts of compassion arise. Usually, however, there is only joy over the spectacle. But if the man who is so pleased were to be led into court, fettered by chains, his joy would in a moment turn into thoughts of unbearable suffering and he would only think of how to become free. Hence, because of this similarity one must turn one's mind inward and meditate on this

---

[1] *Zhl* 22ab.

misery of the whole world as affecting ourselves once we have been born in any form of the six kinds of life.

"When the effect of evil deeds committed through hatred leads to a life in hell, there is at first the feeling of cold in the body, and when one seeks warmth this state of feeling cold vanishes and instead one feels hot and is born in one of the fiery hells. Everywhere the ground is of glowing iron, the enclosure is red-hot iron, and in the midst of flames that leap up all around there is the so-called Reviving Hell. One has to imagine oneself as being born in such a place and one's body must feel agitated all over and one's mind frightened to excess. When one feels this one should think that many beings born there assemble and in an orgy of hatred strike each other with various sharp weapons. One has to imagine this so clearly that one feels how one's body is cut into a hundred thousand pieces and how one is about to swoon. Revived by a voice from the sky which says: 'May you live once more', one must meditate again and again on the suffering of being pierced by swords. When this experience is vividly felt and has a real effect on us, we lose all appetite for food and drink, we do not like idle talk and bustle, and quite naturally we set out to avoid evil and do good in all our ways of living. But if as a result the former mode of acting and behaving is not changed but remains as it was, religion and man become incompatible".

Here it clearly has been stated that the contemplation of the unpleasant states of life is not an end in itself nor a stimulus to action in the narrow sense of the word, but is something that reinforces action towards a goal which is pleasant. Two considerations enter here, man seeks certain experiences because they are pleasant and, still more so, because he needs them. Need is the key to a proper understanding of the place which the contemplation of misery occupies in the whole of man's life. The unpleasant may be likened to a state of tension or disequilibrium which is so characteristic of the functioning of needs. Any form of tension, especially when prolonged, is decidedly unpleasant and its reduction by appropriate action is pleasant. The progress, therefore, is always in the direction of the pleasant. Similarly as the experience of hunger ('the need for food') is unpleasant, the state of a denizen of hell or a spirit deprived of anything that might end its suffering, is the recognition of a need in us, a need for peace and happiness which reinforces and supports the search for that which will fulfil the need.

The fact that the whole of mankind, as far as historical memory extends, has lived religiously, shows that religion has been a basic need and still continues to be so. Religion, as commonly understood, seems to have been intent on embodying its truth in tangible symbols and, in so doing, upon transforming experienced reality into a system of propositions to be taken as literally true. In this development it has been contrasted with philosophy which pursues effective subjective certainty. Religion has symbolized the helpful forces and powers into gods and the evil ones into demons and the Devil, all of which for philosophy is but a medley of deceptive veils and misleading simplifications. Buddhism seems to be more on the philosophical side; it rejects the primitive belief in gods and demons, but as it developed it did not like the 'intellectual' try to kill the primitive within us.

In declaring that the helpful forces are found in The Buddha, The Dharma, and The Sangha, it does not create a new set of gods. It recognizes that man must come to terms with experienced reality by scrutinizing himself and the world much more critically and with much greater regard for facts than for the feelings tangled up with them. Taking refuge in the Three Jewels is the recognition that there is a way to secure happiness and peace, that man can take this way, and that on it he can find help as man to man. In other words, in the field of religious thinking Buddhism never loses sight of man's humanity.

It is important to note that in the whole of Tibetan literature taking refuge is linked with a critical attitude. One does not accept the Buddha or His teaching on mere credulity, but as a result of having examined critically the meaning of the term refuge. Only that which is itself not subject to fear can offer security and only that which is not harmful to others can be a reliable and satisfactory teaching leading to peace, happiness, and spiritual freedom. The Buddha and his teaching fulfil these conditions and in this is found the root of the conception of the Buddha as an idea of man himself as he may become, rather than as an ideal which may break, and of the path becoming a self-disciplinary development of the personality towards the goal of Buddhahood. But this can be realized only at a much higher level of spiritual advancement. Therefore, the taking refuge is done at various levels of spiritual progress and each time the significance becomes more meaningful.

With the certainty that Buddhism does not demand of man that which he cannot reasonably do by himself, man has found a point of view from which he may look at himself and grasp the significance of the relation that holds between his actions and his feelings. Therefore, realizing that good or positive actions ensure happiness and that cruel deeds will bring unhappiness and suffering not only to others but to the perpetrator of the deed as well, man slowly feels the need to avoid those actions which lead to unpleasant consequences. There are ten of them, three belonging to his body, namely murder, theft, and sexual misdemeanour; four to his speech, telling lies, slandering others, speaking words that hurt, and engaging in idle talk; and three to his thought, covetousness, wickedness, and wrong views such as those which deny the relation between the cause and effect of one 's deeds, which disclaim that by following the Buddhist path the goal is reached, or which dismiss the idea of the Three Jewels. The avoidance of these actions is not a passive inactivity but entails a dynamic endeavour to act positively instead. Nor have these ten topics anything to do with commandments, which may or may not be broken with impunity. They are, rather, commitments based on the recognition of the dignity of the human person and deeply felt sympathy for all living beings. Once man begins to think about the possible outcome of his actions, though it still be strongly self-centred, he has set foot on the lowest step of the ladder. He has become an 'inferior' being, inferior in the sense that he has not yet progressed far in his human enterprise.

It needs but little exertion to see that the situation which holds for ourselves can be made to account for the unsatisfactory state we observe everywhere in the world. To a sensitive person the suffering that exists in the world is almost unbearable. The picture of the world that has been developed in Buddhism, may not be 'scientifically' true. The question certainly can never be whether something is 'scientific', but only how it affects us and what is the message it wants to convey to us. The truth to be brought home is that there is no end to suffering if we continue to be driven by our passions. The mythical language depicts in terms of the material the agonies of hell we experience when we succumb to hatred; the morbid craving for things made unattainable by depriving ourselves of the joys of what we have through our greediness and miserliness; the brutishness, ferocity and stubbornness through which we continue to plod on like beasts of burden and prey; the demoniacalness of jealousy and the proud intoxication of godliness, which goes before a fall. This better than any other language reveals the fact that until our emotionality is tamed there will be no end to suffering and conflict. But taming one's emotionality does not mean to repress the emotions. This would only lead to a displacement of their energy and they would frustrate us in other equally destructive forms. To tame them means to recognize them for what they are, and in this recognition they lose their power to take us unaware. Instead of being enemies they become our dearest friends. This transformation process is the theme of and the training that belongs to the period of following the graded path of Tantrism. On this lower level, here, it means first of all to recognize the emotion together with that which makes it arise and then to counteract it by its opposite, the most effective one being to recognize that all emotions are ego-centred and that they become ineffective by the analysis of the nature of the 'I'. Such an analysis necessitates a higher training of the mind and it is here that the idea of interdependent origination finds its application. Just as the positive emotion of love is the best counteragent for the negative one of hatred, so the understanding of relativity, of the concurrence of many circumstances and forces, is the best means to overcome the belief in a self as something that exists absolutely. It should be noted here that Buddhism takes a broader view of emotions than we usually do in psychology. Not only are there positive and negative emotions of feeling, such as passion-lust and aversion-hatred, there is also an 'intellectual' emotion, an un-knowing. While for the Prāsangikas every un-knowing is an emotion, the Svātantrikas distinguished between an emotionally toned un-knowing and an un-knowing not so toned. The content of the former is the belief in the ontological status of an individual self, that of the latter of things other than the self. Belief in an individual self is, according to this distinction, plain wishfulness, that in things other than the self intellectual fog. The Prāsangikas, on the other hand, considered every belief in an ontological status, be it of an individual self or of things other than the self, as wishfulness and emotivity, and that only the tendency to such a belief represented intellectual fog.

The conception of relativity is certainly an advance on the somewhat crude formulation of cause and effect as it pertains to one's actions when held on the level of the inferior person. As William S. Haas rightly remarks [1]: "... only a superficial representation can interpret the relation between actions and their consequences, or between previous and actual existences and the succeeding ones, as determined by the law of causality. Since no soul-substance or anything else substantial is assumed to exist, there is nothing which may be called cause, and nothing where causality could take its start. The relation between the karmatic tendencies or the craving which survive death and their concurrent appearances as rebirth cannot be conceived under the image of cause and effect"! It is with this 'world'-perspective that the status of a 'mediocre' man has been reached.

Having now emerged out of the most narrow confines of ego-centred-

[1] *The Destiny of the Mind. East and West.* London, Faber and Faber, 1956, p. 209.

ness, man, by taking a broader view of himself in a world that owes most of its existence to his marking, can set out on the specific path of his humanity by realizing how his very nature reaches out to others. Therefore, whenever the Buddhist texts, be they those of the dGe-lugs-pas, bKa'-brgyud-pas, rNying-ma-pas or Sa-skya-pas, speak of the course for the superior man, they insist that the contemplation of whatever pertains to the inferior and mediocre types of man must precede any further attempt of self-development, for otherwise no solid foundation has been laid.

These four topics,

1. the uniqueness of human existence,
2. its transitoriness through death,
3. the relation between the cause and effect of one's actions, and
4. the general unsatisfactoriness of the world,

serve as powerful stimulants to the practice of loving-kindness and compassion, when seen against the background of taking refuge in the Buddha as an idea of man, and in his teaching as the path of an inner spiritual development, and in the community of spiritually minded persons as friendly helpers. Indeed, if life is short and suffering is in abundance man must refrain from adding to the existing misery and do whatever he can to alleviate and reduce it. Both loving-kindness and compassion, the one the intention that all sentient beings may feel happy and the other that all sentient beings may be relieved of suffering, serve as forces sustaining an enlightened attitude.

This enlightened attitude is more properly described as a radical change in outlook and a more marked goal-orientation, rather than a fleeting thought of enlightenment. It is usually qualified as 'supreme' or 'precious', and this determination is specifically Mayāyānist. Unlike Hīnayāna the Mahāyāna always recognizes the striving of the Hīnayānist, be he a pious listener or a self-styled Buddha, and frankly admits that without them it would never have come into being. The readiness of the Mahāyānist to take upon himself the responsibility of being active for others finds its expression in the so-called 'perfections'. In a certain sense, however, the current translation by 'perfection' is wrong, because in its abstract sense of faultlessness it suggests the attainment of an ideal. There can be no doubt that ideals have been effective and have influenced our behaviour. This they have done when they were not images of fulfilment, but stimuli to man's desire to rise above himself. The original term, both in Tibetan and Sanskrit (*pha-rol-tu phyin-pa, pāramitā*), always implies this reaching beyond ourselves and the transcending of our ego-centredness. It is therefore obvious that the development of these 'transcending' functions and operations could have originated only in the Mahāyāna which clearly realized that any form of self-centredness is a barrier to communication with others and, since man can find himself best through communication, it is also the greatest hindrance to gaining enlightenment as an awareness that is unbiased and unlimited in its cognition.

The 'six perfections', or, more properly speaking, the six transcending operations are closely related to each other. They are liberality-and-generosity, ethics-and-manners, tolerance-and-patience, strenuousness-and-perseverance, contemplation-and-concentration, and discernment-and-appreciation. I have rendered each transcending operation by two related terms in order to bring out something of the richness of its many meanings. These operations are subsumed under the two ideas of 'fitness of action' and 'intelligence', both of which must unite and constitute the Mayāyānist path *par excellence*. In this conception we clearly recognize that consciousness is inseparable from action or attempted action. To be a thinking person is to have intentions or plans and to try to bring about an effect or achieve a goal. Inasmuch as action is connected with the development of an enlightened attitude or marked goal-consciousness, it will be a help towards our understanding of the specific Buddhist conception when we remind ourselves that there is a kind of knowledge which is intentional and non-propositional and must not necessarily be expressed in verifiable statements. This intentional knowledge implies a certainty about the future course of one's actions. Thus, to work for others (and to know how to go about it) is not a claim of any kind, but a declaration of one's intentions. This is the same as saying that I have made up my mind, and this implies that I have chosen between possible courses of action [1]. 'Intelligence' – (the original term (*shes-rab, prajñā*) is very often translated by 'wisdom' as a sort of wishful thinking) – which is the function which apprehends the real nature of things, always implies analysis, discrimination, appreciation, discernment, and that everything worth mentioning in the performance of an action was intended. As a consequence, 'fitness of action' (*thabs, upāya*) is not just expediency, that is, to do what seems easy, obvious or pleasant; it signifies the best possible course of action in a particular circumstance because of the

---

[1] On this problem in Western philosophy see Stuart Hampshire, *Thought and Action*. London, Chatto and Windus, 1959, pp. 158 seq.

knowledge of the actual situation. The unity of fitness of action and intelligence indicates integration which means that the diverse tendencies in an individual have become harmoniously united. Although it is possible to distinguish between 'fitness of action' and 'intelligence', one must not deal with them in isolation and forget the unity in experience. There is hardly a Mahāyānist text in which this union is not insisted upon: 'intelligence' alone is barren, it needs a moral frame, 'fitness of action'; and the obverse is equally true. The development of an enlightened attitude and the practice of the six transcending operations belong to the level of the 'superior' man. It is the superior man who, if he is particularly gifted, can set out on the path of the Tantras which demand all that is in him and enjoin the strictest self-discipline. And in a certain sense he is bound to set out on this path because it is itself a necessary part of his freedom of thought.

CHAPTER THREE

THE DIVINE IN MAN'S LIFE

Religious thinking, as contrasted with the philosophical quest for knowledge and truth, has often been scorned. This is only justified when, instead of keeping the religious experience alive, it turns into mere idolatry and blocks every attempt to understand what the religious experience means to a person. But apart from this aberration there is nothing to show that religious and critical thinking contradict each other; rather they are mutually compatible and complementary, the one providing the rich, vivid and emotionally moving material which is to be investigated critically and constructively by the other. Religious insight, therefore, is not the sum of the sophisticated expressions and statements of an established 'religion', it is the continuous enquiry into their meaning. To understand religious thinking needs a very sympathetic attitude, never the fatuousness of a supposed superiority and 'objectivity'. As L. A. Reid observes [1]: "The understanding of religion requires very sympathetic study; perhaps it requires more-religion itself. Of any human activity which involves feeling and will – such as art – one must say that in order to understand it one must be rather more than sympathetic to it; one must to some extent be involved in it, even in order (at a different moment) to understand it in a detached way. In trying to understand religion it would seem that one has to go even further. Religion is not one specific activity like art or philosophy; it is a many-sided and total life. Religion, from the side of the subject, is a commitment, a commitment of faith. And there is a sense in which one simply does not understand what it is all about unless one is already committed and can apprehend its meaning from the inside. *Credo ut intelligam.* The intellectual, standing outside religion, scrutinizing with cold neutrality, can in fact see very little

---

[1] *Ways of Knowledge and Experience.* London, George Allen & Unwin Ltd., p. 104.

(except externals – which is perhaps why primitive religions are a favourite hunting ground) of what the believer sees from his side."

Reid's words apply not only to the study of primitive religions, they are of equal force for that of Buddhism and the religion(s) of Tibet in general. Buddhism, above all in its Tantric form, is something that involves the whole man and not merely his brain; hence no understanding is gained by stating a few historical facts (which even may be doubted as facts about the religion under consideration), by failing to distinguish between literalness and symbolicalness as well as to be aware of their close relationship, and by overlooking the most important point, the adequateness of representation. The vital importance of religious thinking is that its ideas guide behaviour and offer encouragement when man needs it most; when he is confronted with obstacles he has to overcome in order to work out a richer and fuller life.

The ideas of religious thinking have a peculiar quality. The divine which they attempt to formulate, has, as W. E. Hocking points out [1], "something in it 'like the fear of ghosts' to make early man more timorous in the world than he would have been without it; and just as evidently it has something in it (like the guardian spirits, totems, fetishes) to give him greater confidence in the world than he would have without it". This double aspect of friendliness and severity, quietness and wrathfulness, which on the 'higher' levels we tend to separate into different categories and entities and thereby destroy the coherence and efficacity of the symbol, is conspicuous, in the divine images depicted in Tibetan art and meditated upon when pursuing the path of self-development. A recurrent qualification is that these deities abolish unfavourable conditions and bring about favourable ones. The unfavourable ones are essentially of an inner nature and are, broadly speaking, all forms of emotional disturbances which with demoniac vehemence throw man off his balance and prevent him from pursuing his path of spiritual development [2].

---

[1] *Types of Philosophy* (Third edition). New York, Charles Scribner's Sons, p. 18.

[2] In *Phbkh* III 3, 3a, these forces are specified as the Four Māras. They are known by their Sanskrit names as Kleśamāra, Skandhamāra, Mṛtyumāra and Devaputramāra. According to *Chz* II 32b seq., "Kleśamāra misleads sentient beings and creates obstacles to the aspirants by making them confused through countless subtle and coarse emotional upsets due to the wrong belief in that which is not a self as being a self. Skandhamāra blocks the way which does not arouse emotive responses and immerses beings in the misery of the three realms in Saṃsāra (the sensuous and sensual world, the world of pure form, and the world of formlessness) by letting them believe in the five psychophysical constituents as a self and

That which is experienced in religious thinking is usually called 'God', but this word itself does not solve any problems, because, as C. D. Broad [1] has shown, it is used in at least three different senses, a popular, a theological, and a philosophical one, all of which at times overlap and very often have associations and arouse emotions which are not justified by what may be considered as facts. Moreover, while we may dismiss the popular sense of 'God' as too naive and the theological one as too dogmatic and doctrinal, even the philosophical one is open to objections. It may be used in the deistic sense, deism being the doctrine that "there is a certain part of the Universe which is not existentially dependent on anything else, and that all the rest of the Universe is existentially dependent on this part of it" [2]. Another use is to apply the term 'God' to the whole Universe as having certain characteristics from which all others necessarily follow. This is a kind of pantheism. Lastly the word 'God' is used to denote those features of the Universe which actually belong to it and are not mere distortions or illusory appearances. On this view the Universe is in reality purely mental and matter, space and motion are distorted appearances of this mind. There is nothing to show that Buddhism falls in with any of these three views. It eschews a First Cause as well as the mentalistic premise that the Universe in its totality is a mind or a society of minds. And it also rejects the thesis that the Universe in all its aspects is God. Therefore, before we speak of God or Gods in Buddhism and jump to the conclusion that it is something polytheistic or that a theistic element has been introduced into it at a later phase of its development we had better find out what the label 'God' (*lha, deva*) means in Buddhism.

The Tibetan term *lha* is used for at least two different conceptions. One refers to one of the six forms of life, all of which are transitory and basically unsatisfactory. The realm of gods differs from that of man in the sense that the gods are happier for longer periods, although for the most part they are morally inferior to man. Their enjoyments are much

---

become involved in Saṃsāra through the affect-arousing organization of these constituents. Mṛtyumāra deprives beings of their life and at improper times and through death interrupts development, studying, thinking about that which one studies, and contemplating it as it bears on one's life not being allowed to come to its end. Devaputramāra comprises Cupid and others". The text then continues to classify these forces as experienced reality.

[1] *Religion, Philosophy, and Psychical Research.* London, Routledge & Kegan Paul Limited, 1953, pp. 159 seqq.

[2] *Ibid.*, p. 165.

the same as those in which most of us temporarily indulge, and a sudden transition from one realm to the other would be hardly noticed as such. There is very little sense in trying to reach this paradise as it merely blunts all one's faculties. According to Buddhism the relative ease with which life goes on in paradise is a handicap for winning enlightenment, not a state of exaltedness as in other religions.

The other use of the term *lha* is to refer to what may be called experiences of 'spiritual forces'. In this sense, 'god' is a mere label for something in which the sense of the transcendent has found utterance and expression. It does not mean that it is a mind. Moreover, these forces are nothing permanent or immortal. They come into being and work during one's spiritual development and it is through them that we become aware of our transcendence and limitation. And since this awareness is so important for man's life, Tantrism teaches man how to find access to this experience again.

All this shows that there is nothing theistic or polytheistic in Buddhism. For theism in religion is, as F.S.C. Northrop [1] has shown, "the thesis that the divine is identified with an immortal, non-transitory factor in the nature of things, which is determinate in character. A theistic God is one whose character can be conveyed positively by a determinate thesis. His nature is describable in terms of specific attributes". It is true that the 'gods' in Buddhism have many specific attributes but these attributes do not exhaust the nature of the god, they are passing ciphers through which we can glean something of the mystery of our being and becoming, all of which can be hinted at but never adequately expressed.

Religious experience is not restricted to certain individuals and occasions. It can, and often does, pervade all phases of human life and may come through such 'ordinary' experiences as love, beauty, danger, fear, and crises. There is a sense in which the transition form one level to another in the course of one's growth can be said to be a crisis in which a religious experience may come about more easily. The large variety of situations, however, makes for different characteristics and the language and imagery necessarily grows richer and richer in content. But in all these cases the symbolic language exists and functions less to make clear prosaic claims to truth than to articulate the emotionally moving content of the religious experience.

---

[1] *The Meeting of East and West. An Inquiry Concerning World Understanding.* New York, The Macmillan Company, 1949, p. 401.

As guiding principles in the course of self-development religious experiences occupy a prominent position in Buddhism and at each level that experience serves to deepen the understanding of the situation in which man finds himself and to remind him of his obligation which is grounded in his humanity. This has been most clearly elaborated by Tsong-kha-pa, who begins his dissertation with an account of man's learning to appreciate the rich experience Tantrism can offer him. He says [1]:

"A person who wants to reach the plane of omniscience quickly must think and plan as follows: In the same way as I have fallen into the ocean of transmigratory existence, so sentient beings who have been and are like my mother have long drifted about in the abysmal sea of the misery of going from birth to birth. The misery of existence in general and that of the three evil forms of life in particular, is extremely harsh and has been there since beginningless Saṃsāra. For this long time all sentient beings have been and are still worn out by emotional excitability and even now they do not see an end of it. Unless they set out on a path that promises them that they can reach their ultimate goal, they will get nowhere even if occasionally they come to higher forms of life. Moreover, if they do not eradicate the root of existence, their un-knowing, they will have to roam about in Saṃsāra through its power and will experience unimaginable suffering. As only Buddhahood can deliver them from this unbearable suffering, the causal situation for its realization namely the established number of ten spiritual levels and five paths [2] as well as their succession in a definite gradation, has been explained many times in the scriptures of the Pāramitāyāna.

"Moreover, to reach there it is necessary to store merits and acquire knowledge over a period of thirty-three, seven or three 'countless aeons'. Then, having properly prepared our mind by this ordinary path we have to set out on the Guhyamantra path, the ford for the fortunate ones, the most excellent course in self-development, and the specific path providing the knowledge of how to reach the citadel of Vajradhara in a single lifetime.

"It needs the growth of a special certainty about this path which, in many Tantras and authoritative writings, and by the great accomplished sages, has been said to have the power to make us realize the plane of Vadjradhara in seven or sixteen existences, or in the intermediate state between death and rebirth, or in this very life. As certain people have

---

[1] *Tskhp* II 2, 307a seq.

[2] See below Chapter IV.

remarked: If a person who is not suited for the teaching of the Tantras, simply ignores them in spite of there being such a profound path, and merely busies himself with logic and epistemology, he has no chance of setting out on this profound path, and still less is able to make an experience of it. And should he not have heard about it, he is deprived of any opportunity to reach Vajradhara in innumerable 'countless aeons'.

"It will also not do to follow any ordinary path, for our mind needs to be prepared by the path of the three types of man, while detachment, an enlightened attitude, and an unbiased outlook have to be cultivated especially. As to the latter we have to try our best to adopt the view of Nāgārjuna and his disciple (Āryadeva) both of whom have been predicted by the Exalted One in many Sūtras and Tantras. And it also will not do just to set out on the Vajrayāna path: if we want to reach the citadel of Vajradhara quickly we must bring about a harmony between the life forces of the path, i.e., the Guru, the tutelary deity, and the spiritual protectors, and our aim or intention of procedure.

"Moreover, we must know well the specific motivating forces for the attainment of the two aspects of the goal, the cognitive and communicative ones, and let them grow and develop within us. Here also, although it is the special feature of the Anuttarayogatantra to teach how an ordinary person, born from a womb, possessing six constituting elementary forces [1], and being constrained by five fetters [2], can obtain Buddhahood in a single life-time, we must turn to and depend on Guhyasamāja, Cakrasamvara, and Vajrabhairava if we want to reach the citadel of Vajradhara as quickly as possible."

In a highly technical language Tsong-kha-pa then describes the special techniques and experience intensities which are the subject matter of the *Guhyasamājatantra* and the *Cakrasamvaratantra*. The former is classified as a so-called Father-Tantra because it stresses the operational side, while

---

[1] They are: solidity, cohesion, temperature, structure, motility, and creativity. Another classification is: bones, marrow, fertility as deriving from the father, and flesh, skin, blood as deriving from the mother. Inasmuch as Tantrism is essentially a process of spiritual regeneration, described in the symbols of the physical, this process has been elaborated in terms of psycho-biology. See, for instance, *KsNzh* by the famous Amdo Lama dbYangs-can dga'-ba'i blo-gros. Tantrism has anticipated the doctrine that motility is the cradle of the mind, a theory which now has been commonly accepted in psychology. See C. Judson Herrick, *The Evolution of Human Nature*, Austin. University of Texas Press, 1956, pp. 240, 282, 312-318.

[2] The five fetters of emotivity are: passion-lust, hatred-aversion, bewilderment-unknowing, pride-conceitedness, and jealousy-envy.

the latter is a so-called Mother-Tantra because it emphasizes the noetic-appreciative side of the experience. It is, however, important to note that neither of these two Tantras is in any way one-sided, both features, the operational and noetic ones, intermingle [1]. For this reason symbol representations are mostly in the male-female form, the conjugal embrace being the unique way in which a person can achieve the closest spiritual unity with another. Since in the 'Father-Tantra' the operational or 'male' element dominates, while the appreciative or 'female' one is merely hinted at and implied, in artistic representations the female partner wears clothes. In the 'Mother-Tantra' where the appreciative-cognitive or 'female' element is pre- eminent, the female partner is in the nude.

It is the general feature of growth that the individual's attitudes and traits tend to become organized into larger value systems or frames of reference which help man to adapt to his cultural and spiritual world. There are, doubtless, a variety of such fundamental frames of reference or *leitmotifs* which more and more dominate and characterize man's whole life. Thoughts and behaviour may seem unique and particular to a given level within the three types of man, but behind this diversity lies some basic unity-theme which throughout serves as an integrating and co-ordinating focus for a wide range of specific activities which may have their own peculiar, though subsidiary *leitmotifs*. This over-arching unity-theme is known as a *yi-dam*. Its explanation is that it gives mental stability, and only in this sense has the current translation of this term by, 'tutelary deity' any justification. Essentially it is the idea of what man wants to become and achieve, all of which comes to him in an image that arouses him to action and to which he feels himself irresistibly drawn. Therefore, to turn to a *yi-dam* and to depend on him means to be clear about one's goal which as a *leitmotif* will recur in various stages of his development, like the theme that gradually unfolds in a musical symphony.

Tsong-kha-pa then continues:

"In order to experience the Development and Fulfilment Stages [2] as detailed in the *Cakrasamvaratantra* and the *Guhyasamājatantra*, we must depend on the *yi-dam* Vajrabhairava who dispels unfavourable conditions and brings about favourable ones and quickly grants the highest and

---

[1] *Tskhp* V 2, 17b seq.; 25b seq. *Khg* VII 2, 60a seq.

[2] The Developing Stage is the process of regeneration and transfiguration, the Fulfilment Stage is the deep contentment and awareness in the Developing Stage, both of which ultimately unite.

commonest attainments. He has five special features which are not found with others.

"(1) One such feature has often been described in such works as the *'Jam-dpal rtsa-rgyud* (*Mañjuśrīmūlatantra*), the *gSang-ba spyi-rgyud* (*Sarvamaṇḍala-sāmānyavidhīnāṃ guhyatantra*), the *Phyag-na gtum-chung-gi rgyud* and others to the effect that, if in this evil age which is worse than ever and where one is oppressed by obstacles through evil spirits, walking corpses, spectres of the dead, wicked demons, temper-arousing goblins, and false 'leaders' [1], sentient beings do not depend on this *yi-dam* they will be unable to travel the profound path to its end. Such beings are characterized as lazy, of little intelligence, not keeping their commitments, knowing no restraint, harbouring abominably false views, deluded in analyzing the meaning of the scriptures, irreverent towards their spiritual teachers and friends, having little compassion, neither self-respect nor decorum, are puffed up with pride in having rejected religion, arrogant because of their fallacious views and deeply immersed in the morass of bad views, are drunken with the enjoyment of sensual pleasures, short-lived and without merits. Therefore, it is by depending on Vajrabhairava and practising meditation four times a day that they will get rid of these impediments and quickly reach their goal, the citadel of Vajradhara.

"For example when one wants to fetch jewels from an island in the sea it may do to set out in a ship, but it is much better to join an experienced and intelligent captain, who has travelled the route and can be trusted. Then, when one sets out with him in a ship and trusts him on the currents and colour of the sea, the navigation of the ship, the distance of the passage, the suitability of the voyage, and the rocks and rivers, through his efficiency one will quickly obtain the jewels, banish poverty and get whatever one wants.

"The specific feature of this *yi-dam* is that the goal or the citadel of Vajradhara is reached quickly when, by meditating on him, we experience the Development and Fulfilment Stages.

"It may be asked whether the experience as pointed out in the Father- and Mother-Tantras are not ultimately valid and directed towards fulfilment or whatever their nature may be. I will answer this point as I have understood it by the light of Mañjughoṣa's knowledge.

"Although each Tantra, be it the *Cakrasamvaratantra*, the *Guhyasamājatantra*, the *Kālacakratantra*, or the *Hevajratantra*, has its own

[1] According to *Chz* II 33b seq., these are forces which bring about mental depression and also physical illness.

special merits of understanding reality, Vajrabhairava sums up all that has been said in the Father-and Mother-Tantras such as the *Sampuṭa*.

"(II) This second specific feature of uniting the Father-and Mother-Tantras is evident from his symbolism. Thus by holding entrails in one of his hands and a brazier in another he points to the apparitional nature of existence and the radiancy of the knowledge of reality as discussed in the *Guhyasamājatantra* [1].

"(III) The third specific feature is that by brandishing the Khaṭvānga (a staff with three heads one upon the other) he points to the bliss that is felt as spreading when a frozen mind is melted in the fire of meditation. This symbol is not found in any Father-Tantra. It indicates the unity of bliss and no-thing-ness as discussed in the *Cakrasamvaratantra*.

"(IV) His fourth specific feature is that he holds a fire-pot, raises a threatening finger, and carries a man impaled on a stake. These three symbols are not found in any other Tantra.

"The fire-pot is the symbol of his superior discrimination and understanding.

"The threatening finger orders the gods of this world and the ones beyond to listen to him and it means that the ultimate essence of both the Father-and Mother-Tantras is with him. Therefore, if he can threaten the gods of the worlds beyond why cannot he conquer the demons in the ten directions, above and below the earth?!

"The symbol of a man impaled on a stake shows that enlightenment is possible even among evildoers such as those who engage in the ten evil deeds, reject religion, and commit unpardonable crimes [2]. Yet there is a marked difference between this symbol and that of a cremation ground. The latter concerns a mere corpse, this symbol a living individual.

"(V) His fifth and last specific feature is the following: It is very important to rely on Mañjughoṣa when one strives for Buddhahood, as he is the father of all Buddhas. Mañjughoṣa manifests in the wrathful forms

---

[1] The relation between entrails and apparitional existence, on the one hand, and fire-pot and radiancy, on the other, is that apparitional existence is a term for non-essentiality. Through the analysis of all phenomena all essentialist notions have been repudiated; 'essence' has been taken out of them, just as entrails can be taken out of the body. Radiancy is a term for the cognitive awareness of no-thing-ness which can be found in every thing, similar to a fire in a brazier.

[2] This does not mean that any criminal is already a Buddha or a saint. However, if a person learns from the faults and crimes he has committed and in learning his lesson atones for them, the way to spiritual development is opened. The idea of eternal damnation is incompatible with the compassion for every being in Buddhism. Compassion is the very foundation of Mahāyāna Buddhism.

of the Red and Black Yamāntaka and the terrible Vajrabhairava. As a result his alertness and discrimination is much greater than it would be if he had remained as himself, because the manifestation, Vajrabhairava, has been deputized, as it were, to assist the aspirant during the periods of his beginning, his goal-attainment, and his spiritual activity.

"His two horns symbolize the starting point or the two truths (conventional and ultimate), the path or fitness of action and intelligence, and the goal or the two existential patterns (cognitive and communicative). From among the many manifestations who act as deputies and who are discussed in other Sūtras and Tantras, this protector of religion, dispelling unfavourable conditions and bringing about favourable ones, is the most comprehensive one.

"As it is important to follow the graded path of the three types of man, discussed before, the inferior man will have to think that, since he will not be here for long, he will have to take into account transitoriness through death, the relation between the cause and effect of his actions, the general unsatisfactoriness of the world, and the fact that the only power that can protect him from these vicissitudes is that of taking refuge in the Three Jewels. In order to feel that which he is contemplating, he must turn to the King of the law, Yamāntaka, who is also called Lord of death, Witness of good and evil, Punisher of the wicked, Rewarder of the good, the Mirror revealing the relation between the cause and effect of man's actions, and King of the law because he decides according to that which is good and evil or because he acts in accordance with the law. He is also called Karma-Yamāntaka, because he is judge and witness of positive and negative deeds.

"As all this belongs to the level of an inferior person, a man who is on this level has to depend on this Karma-Yamāntaka in order to gain a vivid experience of his situation.

"The dominant idea of the mediocre man is that it is not only necessary to find the means for a happy state of being, but that one must be active finding deliverance through detachment, because one sees the infinite worlds to be a flaming pit. The vision of the futility of the world, and the consequent achievement of the feeling of disgust with it and detachment of oneself from it, is the main subject of the training in that which is considered to be ethically commendable. As a matter of fact, ethics and detachment mean the same. Here one has to turn to King Vaiśravaṇa, for he is the guardian of the disciplinary code among the three sections of the Buddhist scriptures, the guardian of training in the ethically commendable.

"The superior being is not concerned with finding deliverance from the world for himself alone, he develops an enlightened attitude in order to deliver all sentient beings, who have been and are like his mother, from the ocean of misery in Saṃsāra. In order to be alert for this task and to know how to go about it he must rely on the 'Speeder', the great Black Lord of Transcending Awareness (Mahākāla), who has six arms and who is a manifestation of Avalokiteśvara (the symbol of the Buddha's Great Compassion).

"Inasmuch as the path of fitness of action and intelligence must develop in us, we must rely on this Lord in order to bring to life this enlightened attitude, especially as he is the 'compassionate' protector of religion.

"And in order to develop discrimination or an unbiased outlook we must rely on Yamāntaka, King of the law, because he is the 'discerning' protector of religion, a deputy of Mañjughoṣa (symbolizing discernment as it operates on the Buddha-level)".

The varying symbolism on the levels described in this significant passage, corresponds to and reflects our growth. First of all, on the lowest level, we have to develop our sense of discrimination which is the anticipation of the goal of all our endeavours, the realization of unbounded cognition in pure experience. The development of this capacity then leads to restraint and opens us to others through compassion which is the necessary prerequisite for an enlightened attitude and which can operate only when its foundation has been laid by the experience of the previous levels and the lessons they teach us.

There is doubtless a considerable amount of anthropomorphism and mythical thinking involved here, which is unacceptable to many a 'modern' mind who would like to substitute for it 'timeless truths' which precisely because of their timelessness have no meaning to man in time. Another objection that is likely to be raised is that all these gods are doing temporal acts. If it is really true, as theologians claim, that the Divine is non-temporal, how can we ascribe temporal processes and qualities to that which is non-temporal without becoming involved in endless contradictions? This difficulty does not exist for a Buddhist, as he does not think in terms of 'things' and their 'qualities', but in terms of dynamic processes which, by virtue of their dynamics and variability, are vivid and therefore 'divine'. The gods are functions and their formulations in concrete forms are symbols for the inner experiences that attend man's spiritual growth. Even if a person may not be able to describe the feelings which prompted the birth of these symbols, they will be intelligible to anyone who has had the experience which called them forth.

It is the very nature of every living symbol that, on the one hand, it clamours for an interpretation. This, in a certain sense, is an advance on the symbol itself inasmuch as it becomes conceptual and, since concepts are the stock we use in thinking, we thereby are enabled to understand ourselves, our relation to the world in which we live, and our adjustment to our cultural and spiritual world is facilitated. The danger in this process of interpreting the symbol is that its comprehensive content becomes diluted, thin and fragmentized and so loses much of its emotionally moving power. As a consequence, thinking conceptually may become sterile and barren leading to utter emotional and spiritual starvation. On the other hand, symbols, if they are genuine and not desymbolized signs, tend to point beyond themselves and incite to further symbol-thinking and an enrichment of the personality, because man's highest endeavours to express what he feels not only as a presence, but also as a need, demand symbols.

Although it is important to distinguish between the literal and the symbolical, there is always an irreducible core of literalness in the symbol. If the divine presence is not 'there' and if we cannot communicate with it or if it does not 'speak' to us, the whole basis of religious symbolism and religious experience is taken away from under us. On the other hand, the symbolic element is as irreducible and unavoidable as the literal one. In its dramatic setting we may speak of religious language as myth-making, and as L. A. Reid has demonstrated, "we have to use various forms of mythological language because we cannot express the transcendent and our sense of it in any other way. We can of course to some extent do so in abstract language of concepts. But as we know, this is extremely thin in content, it tends to be negative; and even abstract language (like 'transcendence' itself) strains towards metaphor. Religious (as distinct from theological and philosophical) language is essentially metaphorical, mythicogenic, mythic and even myth-making because man's highest endeavours to express divine things demand all this "[1].

Every kind of thinking consists in anticipating one's own actions and those of others. It has a dramatic character which is aptly described as an 'inner forum' on which social acts are performed. Such an inner forum it technically known as a *maṇḍala*. It has a centre which, like a power centre, uniformly spreads into all directions of the compass and, since the centre is the individual himself, this spread into all directions indicates man's orientation in the world. On the whole four degrees have been

[1] *Ways of Knowledge and Experience*, p. 153.

recognized and symbolized by four different colours. Thus white stands for the pacificatory and quiet activity, yellow for an expanding and enriching quality, red for majesticalness which, however, is attractive rather than subjugating, and blue-black for the forcible aspect of action [1]. The varying qualities may overlap, as for instance the majestic and forcible, which then is expressed by the colour green.

However important the centre of the *maṇḍala* may be, it never occurs in a vacuum. The god lives in a palatial mansion, just as man lives in a house; and in the same way as the latter directs his actions, be they pacificatory or forcible, to the various parts of his 'world' and communicates with others, men and women, so the god expands and 'deputizes' his entourage of gods and goddesses. The character of the inner forum with its enactment of social acts expresses itself in the communion and interaction between males and females, and the closenesss of this interaction is symbolically represented by the conjugal embrace of the gods and goddesses. This is *not* because we want to elevate our ordinary conduct, which may range from a casual sex attraction to a total relationship of two persons in which the physical and spiritual form an indivisible unity, but because the revelation of the divine and transcendent comes to us in earthen vessels.

The marked difference between our 'ordinary' social acts and those enacted within the world of the *maṇḍala*, is that the former are mostly concerned with a world of things where even persons have been degraded into things to be used and manipulated for a certain purpose, while here the interaction takes place between subjects. The contemplation of the *maṇḍala* is thus a projection of one's inner life which reflects back on the subject by bringing about the first dawning of the fact that man's being is not narrowly circumscribed like that of a thing, but stretches out ahead of himself so that he decides the nature of the world in which he lives. This awareness leads him to recognize the importance of the very moment. He realizes that he must act in such a way that if death should strike him now, his life will have been significant and worth-while.

To be compelled to decide here and now is a highly dramatic situation which is not without an element of fear. The object of this fear is not an innerworldly threat, but man's whole existence which may be undone in a moment. To decide is therefore never an isolated event locked up inside of a subject. It refers to a world of things and, above all, of subjects and involves an ordering of the world. Similarly, to decide is also not an

---

[1] *Tskhp* VI 1, 64a.

accident added to something already existing and by itself immutable. To decide is the very life of man and from his decisions his actions will spread. Thus, the *maṇḍala* as the visible and emotionally moving expression of the drama of decision and as the incentive for enacting this drama anew, is unique because, in its nature as being evocative of a divine world and of the divine presence felt by the individual who turns to the divine for guidance and support, it gives man access to a world which he needs and which he yet loses again and again. Although man alone must decide the course of his being and becoming, he is not alone at this critical moment.

It is true to say that it is all myth to speak of Yamāntaka as 'King of the law', 'Punisher of the wicked', 'Rewarder of the good', or to describe him as a deputy of Mañjughoṣa who is the symbol and embodiment of all Buddha-knowledge, or as operating on the lowest level of man's development through his fearful form of 'Lord of death'. And yet what this myth wants to impress on us is vital. Every growth and progress is a kind of dying, but before something can die in us we, as it were, must die with it so that something greater and richer may be born. A man who passes through this drama may well be said to have come to possess deeper and deeper insight. L. A. Reid, in assessing the value of mythic thinking in religion, remarks: "There is mythic thinking here, and it is necessary. It is not the end or the last word, but only one way in which we physically bodied creatures can live intensely our spiritual life" [1].

The situation changes when the level of the mediocre man is attained. Here assistance is gained from Vaiśravaṇa whose symbolism with its predominance of yellow and white points to an unfolding of wealth. All the gods who are under his rule have to do with riches. This means that the mood of the situation is a feeling of expansion and enrichment, rather than one of fear which attends our decisions. Inasmuch as here, too, the person's growth and spiritual development is important, enrichment is to be understood as an inner process of enhancement of values, not as a craving 'to make money and grow rich'. This inner enrichment is intimately related to the observance of that which is ethically commendable. This implies restraint from evil and commitment to positive actions out of which the obligation to assist others in their spiritual quest is the natural consequence. Restraint has a stabilizing effect on the person who practises it, while the commitment to positive actions lets all that

[1] *Ways of Knowledge and Experience*, p. 147.

which is necessary and helpful for goal-attainment mature within the person. Through this process, by which I myself become aware of my own spiritual needs, my understanding of the needs of others is also made possible and instead of engaging in sentimental actions which do more harm than good because they are grounded in the ignorance of the actual requirement, I am in a position to help others by giving them the chance to let that which is necessary for them mature in them.

Here, too, the symbolism of the 'King of wealth' is suggestive in its literalness. The 'king' administers justice and upholds order and discipline; and in the experience of the binding force of ethics and obligation I recognize a value relevant to my concrete existence which can prosper only in a condition of orderliness. In the search of all that makes life worth-while and valuable men turn to ethics and moral philosophy which promise them disciplined help. However, such help is not forthcoming if I gaze abstractly at standards which are divorced from my actual plight and which fail to account for my feeling of being under an obligation to act in a certain way or which, since men try to justify themselves as they are as well as for what they have done, also fail to account for this urge for justification as rooted in the specific nature of man. The help which man needs is won through the awareness and feeling of existing in ordered activity. And this certainly is an enrichment of the person just as conversely a life of disorder entails frustration and impoverishment.

Again the situation changes when the level of the superior man is reached. Compassion, which is the predominant feature of this type of man, is essentially the intention that all beings may be delivered from misery. The forces of misery that depress man and block his self-development are immense, and forcible endeavour has to be made more than ever to overcome them. No wonder that the guiding principle should be the 'Black Lord of Transcendent Awareness', because compassion unsupported by knowledge is a mere sentimentality, that leads to nothing and leaves the person on whom it is showered, as destitute and miserable as he was before.

All that which is not and cannot be clearly understood as it rises out of the depth of the psychic life of man, and which not only disturbs but also frequently dominates him, has been concretely formulated as 'demons'. Where these demons are not a mere figure of speech they are the vivid expression of man's active engagement in experienced reality, as it is felt in horror or ecstasy. This feeling that what we can sense points to something hidden, unfathomable, and demonic, strikes us irresistibly. But to succumb without understanding it, leads to fragmentation. This happens especially when the 'demons' become absolutized as in superstition and aestheticism, where man is at the mercy of his passions and sentiments. It is therefore of utmost importance to destroy these fragmentizing tendencies. But to do so is to recognize them for what they are. This recognition is both spiritual nourishment ('food for thought') and the death of all that which tends to starve man by preventing him from finding himself. In symbol representations Mahākāla, the 'Black Lord of Transcending Awareness', wields a flaming dagger with which to cut the thread of life of these demons, and holds a skull brim-full with their brain substance which he pours into his mouth.

Compassion, and especially 'Great Compassion', which is conspicuous by its absence in most of us who nevertheless would like to be considered superior types of man, has "as its special cause and antecedent the practice of loving-kindness throughout many aeons, as its actuality, – (in other words) one feels the plight of any sentient being as acutely as if one's leg were hit by a sharp weapon. As its effect it has the capacity of developing the noble intention of always being ready (to help) others" [1]. This compassion extends to all the six kinds of beings. However, in order to perform its task it must be equal to the cognition underlying and accompanying it. This is achieved in goal-attainment which is the unity of the cognitive, communicative and manifestation patterns realized in Buddhahood. To show that the goal has been reached and that this compassion covers all sentient beings struggling in the six forms of life, Mahākāla, the 'Black Lord of Transcendent Awareness', holds in his second pair of hands a trident symbolic of the three patterns of goal-attainment, and a rosary of skulls symbolic of his action which leads all sentient beings out of their state of misery. For the skull itself is a symbol of transitoriness through death and reminds us of our obligation to show compassion to those who are in the clutches of death.

Lastly, in his third pair of hands he holds a drum summoning all powers to obey him and a leash with which to fetter those who might undo the unificatory and developmental process [2].

Against the background of these diverse realms of action and at the base of all our spiritual activity one unifying force is working. This is not to say that it exists outside of ourselves or has a being of its own apart from us; it resides in the maintenance and development of this

---

[1] *Ktsh* 170b-171a.

[2] This symbolism is based on *Tchks* 3a seqq.

unity. Though not in essence something special or distinct from the unity-themes so far considered, its peculiar feature is that it sets off many short-run activities such as those belonging to each of the three levels of personality, all of which however are directed to the goal or long-time end. However important the knowledge of our goal may be, it is of no concern if it is merely nominal or a purely intellectual apprehension. Knowledge of the goal must be felt and such a feeling is aided by the symbol, while in the search for one's goal both symbolism and abstract propositions must go together. Felt knowledge of man's spiritual growth through all its phases, is expressed in the image of Vajrabhairava. He may be contemplated as being single or in the embrace with his spouse; and the difference is that through the former symbolism he points to the cognitive act as it is grounded in the knowing subject, while through the latter to the fulfilment of that which in purely philosophical terms is called 'noetic identity' or 'cognitive union' and of which I have spoken before. However, to speak of it thus in the abstract, in strictly objective scientific terms, is precisely to leave out the feeling component, the 'involvement', the 'existential' and 'felt' knowledge which alone has any significance for man in his noetic quest. The symbol representation which uses the physical and even the physiological as its vehicle must be regarded not merely as physical or physiological, but always as expressive of meaning. Meaning is not a constructed intellectual scheme (but neither is it anti-intellectual nor anti-rational); it is a personal acquisition, the growing and deepening insight of a thinking, feeling, and acting person through intellectual, emotional, and moral experiences, all of which are not so many separate items, but the unity of a total life.

The 'meaning' of the symbols which gradually dawns upon him who contemplates and immerses himself in Vajrabhairava, is that "his nine faces point to the ninefold classification of the scriptures [1]; his two horns to the two truths (conventional and ultimate); his thirty-four arms together with his spirituality, communication and embodiment in tangible form to the thirty-seven facets of enlightenment [2]; his sixteen legs to the sixteen kinds of no-thing-ness [3]; his erect penis to the unfolding of bliss; the human being and the other mammals on which he stands, to

---

[1] Sūtra, Geya, Vyākaraṇa, Gāthā, Udāna, Itivṛttaka, Jātaka, Adbhutadharma, and Vaipulya.

[2] See p. 87.

[3] They are enumerated in *Madhyāntavibhāgaṭīkā*, pp. 43 seq., 51 seq. Other texts mention twenty varieties. They all relate to possible implications of the non-existence of things in truth.

the eight attainments; the eagle and the other birds on which he tramples, to the eight surpassing strengths [1]; his nakedness to his being undefiled by emotional upsets and by intellectual fogs; his hair which stands on end to the citadel that is beyond all worries. In brief, the thirty-seven facets of enlightenment are the path through which one gains the inner experience of the conventional as being like an apparition and of the ultimate being as limitless as celestial space, both of which are the subject matter or the ninefold classification of the scriptures and provide a basis for one's setting out on the path. The main purpose of this path is the intuitive apprehension of the ultimate, and this is the understanding of the sixteen kinds of no-thing-ness. This, however, is indivisible from the feeling of great bliss as instrumentality. The goal that is reached by travelling this path, its essential feature being the common and specific attainments, is beyondness in which neither emotional excitability nor intellectual fog obtains "[2].

---

[1] The eight attainments and eight strengths refer to Buddha-qualities and Buddha-activities. The former indicate mental stability, the latter unbiased awareness and activity.

[2] *Phbkh* III 3, 16a seqq. The same explanation of the symbols is given in *Khg* VII 3, 91b seq. Although this description refers to Vajrabhairava when single, it also applies when he has united with his spouse. As detailed on fol. 19a of the above mentioned work, the sexual symbolism refers to the incipient union with no-thing-ness, which happens through 'great bliss'. The latter is never a physiological tension release. This is plainly stated in all texts on this subject matter. When certain scholars speak of an 'eroticized' form of Buddhism, blowing the trumpets of righteous indignation, they merely advertize their ignorance of the symbol language. As is emphasized in *Tskhp* XI 12, 5b, in order to enjoy the pleasure of sleeping with a woman no instruction by a Guru as to the significance of 'great bliss' is necessary. Therefore, the less is said about such absurd theories, even if they have been held by very learned men, the better it is.

CHAPTER FOUR

THE PATH AND THE GOAL

When Buddhism declares that it is a path leading to a goal that is realizable by man, it always insists on knowledge born of the desire to cultivate and refine the personality and of the need to find deliverance, both of which go together and are deeply felt as they develop and grow in the individual. In recent times these two kinds of knowledge have been pushed more and more into the background so as to give preference to knowledge which aims at domination over external nature and at streamlining individual thought and action into rigidly fixed mass patterns. As a consequence, philosophers who have been fascinated by the obvious achievements of science, have felt tempted to restrict knowledge to a discursive treatment of diverse subjects and to barren statements that something is the case. Such a narrow view (narrow because there are many meanings to 'knowledge' all of which are important as they contribute to its unique valuableness) ignores the growing sense of vital insecurity. It fails completely to account for the ever-present quest for that kind of knowledge which, even if it does not conform to the discursive pattern and to the shallow chatter by which anything can be said in such a way that nothing significant has been said, bears on human existence as a whole, makes for contentment and happiness and enables man to lead a richer life. There is certainly a good deal of feeling in this kind of knowledge, but it would be a grave mistake to dismiss it as mere 'feeling somehow'. Indeed, this would be a dangerous misinterpretation and nothing but sentimentalism and emotionalism could come out of it. Feelings are never purely subjective sensations that are pleasant or unpleasant, they are transitive in the sense that they constantly reveal the situation of which I am the centre and, above all, how it is going with me, which is so important in pursuing the path of self-development and spiritual growth. The unity of feelings and cognitions is always implied by the Buddhist 'path', where path is a comprehensive term for what in abstract language we call goal-consciousness and goal-directed striving and development [1]. However, as has been pointed out before, there are considerable differences in the ideas about what the goal is to be, even if all Buddhist schools of thought agree that deliverance and the well-integrated personality are the main objectives. In Hīnayāna, deliverance means freedom from emotional upsets which are considered to be the main cause for man becoming involved in Saṃsāra, for continuously being driven from one existence to another with no independence because he is in the grip of his passions which he cherishes instead of examining them critically. Here the integrated personality is the Arhant or saintly sage who, as the indigenous interpretation of the word shows, 'has slain the foe' of whishfulness and emotivity. As this goal-conception is extremely self-centred it has a strong quietistic, if not negative, flavour and therefore has become the target of the Mahāyānist critique.

For the Mahāyānist the goal is nothing less than the attainment of Buddhahood for the sake of all sentient beings so as to be able to help them to find their way to the goal, which always remains a personal achievement and is never a fortuitous gift or an unmerited favour. Buddhahood, negatively speaking, is the elimination of everything emotionally upsetting, not only in its actuality but, even more important, in its latency, as well as the removal of every kind of all intellectual fog. Positively speaking, it is the attainment of everything ennobling and, in particular, the realization of those existential norms which are active and dynamic ways of being, rather than determinate traits and properties fixed once for all. While the Mahāyānists agree on this idea of Buddhahood, there are again considerable differences in that which is to be counted as emotional disturbances and as intellectual fog.

Buddhism has always been a dynamic way of thinking and therefore has rejected any static conception of man and the universe. Throughout its history it has denied the validity of ontology because it clearly saw that, although ontology pretends to be a doctrine of being itself as such, it has always turned out to be the doctrine of a particular being within Being. Out of this recognition and conviction the Prāsangikas considered that any belief in an ontological status of a self or of a thing other than the self is an emotional disturbance, while the belief in any such ontological postulate as something existing in truth or being the last word in philosophical thinking is intellectual fog. More precisely, it is the tendency to such a belief that constitutes intellectual fog, the actual belief already

---

[1] The contents of this chapter are based on *SLNzh* by dKon-mchog 'Jigs-med dbang-po; *SLSHp* by bsTan-pa dar bzang; and *Khg* VII 8.

partaking of emotivity. For the Svātantrikas the belief in an ontological status of a self is wishfulness and emotivity, while intellectual fog is the belief in the ontological status of things other than the self, as well as the belief in anything, be this a self or an object of nature, as existing in truth. And for the Vijñānavādins belief in a self is emotivity, and belief in things as existing apart from their being experienced, constitutes intellectual fog.

Whether we speak of the Hīnayānists' path as travelled by Srāvakas (pious listeners) and Pratyekabuddhas (self-styled Buddhas), or of the Mahāyānist's one as traversed by the superior type of man, the path begins when the need to find deliverance and sainthood or Buddhahood, as the case may be, is really felt by the individual. In Mahāyāna the path opens simultaneously with the development of an enlightened attitude, rooted in unbounded compassion or the intention that all sentient beings may be freed from suffering. Such an attitude reflects the beginning of a marked change in the personality as it indicates the shift from self-centred isolation to wider communication with others. Above all it is the decision to follow a human and humane road. In Hīnayāna the path unfolds when the individual begins to detach himself from his preoccupation with worldly (and transworldly) affairs by having seen all these projects to be like a blazing fire that threatens to consume the last trace of his humanity.

This Buddhist path of self-development, which culminates in an integrated personality and in the deliverance from outer and inner obstacles, comprises five stages, each of which is termed a 'path', because it leads to and merges in the subsequent phase as its goal. The path is therefore not an inert rod linking two equally inert terms, but a pervasive process. The first four phases or 'paths' are called 'the path of learning'. Its first two stages, 'the preparatory path' and 'the connecting path', belong to the level of the ordinary person, while the third and fourth stages, 'the path of seeing' and 'the path of attending to the seen', can only be travelled by the advanced person who ultimately sets out on the 'path of no more learning' and realizes his goal.

Learning begins with the acquisition of knowledge, which is always knowledge as it bears on human existence. This implies the use of one's intelligence (though not in the sense of an ability to perform tests that can be measured quantitatively and expressed as a percentage. Such a conception of intelligence ranks very low because, more often than not, persons with a high IQ are utterly unintelligent where there humanity is involved). 'Existential' knowledge is acquired in a social environment, and this social aspect is indicated by the 'acquisition of merits'. Both merits and existential knowledge reinforce each other and are futile if the individual who stores them fails to gain insight and understanding of his humanity. The moment when we feel goal-conscious and become aware of our humanity is called 'the preparatory path', because we are ready to respond, perceive, think and feel in a rather persistent and particular way towards an object. In other words, since in mapping out the road of our becoming we do not become aware of objects but of projects, we are ready to deal with these projects in which we objectify ourselves as we are going to be, while at the same time being aware of ourselves as acting and thinking. As a deeply felt concern with a value it is an incentive to sustained action and this leads to the second stage, 'the connecting path'.

This second stage is so called because it connects the initial readiness to attain a goal with the actual approach to it, which is a growing insight the object of which varies according to the goal-conception of Śrāvakas, Pratyekabuddhas and Bodhisattvas. This 'connecting path' is marked by a release of 'warmer' feelings which serve to reinforce mental life and conduct. Although it is here that the elimination of wishfulness and emotivity, and in the case of the Mahāyānists also of intellectual fog, begins in the sense that these dominating forces lose strength, this loss does not, as is often assumed, lead to a state of emotional undernourishment and intellectual blankness. Rather it produces a heightened perceptivity and responsiveness which is all the more satisfactory because the disturbing and upsetting elements are in the course of being eliminated. Four degrees of intensity are distinguished and its comparison with fire shows that the warmer feelings that are released give added strength to the process already under way.

As a pervasive process this 'connecting path' initiates 'the path of seeing' which is the most decisive event in the course of development. The four intensity degrees of the 'connecting path' are called 'warmth' because the frozenness of one's self-centredness is gradually melting and, as the texts declare, warmth is the sign that fire has been kindled. 'Before this warmth sets in, whatever there may be of the good and wholesome is likely to be destroyed by anger and emotional outbreaks, but when the 'peak value' (the second intensity degree) of this fire has been reached no good can be destroyed. One speaks of a 'peak value' because like a fire the good and wholesome leaps up into a tapering flame. This is also said to be the attainment of a level which is beyond the hazard of good being destroyed. The newly won acceptance of reality which is not afraid of its being no-thing-ness, the profound nature of reality, is called 'patient acceptance'. It is also said to be the attainment of a state beyond the misery of passing through unhappy forms of life which are created by the power of actions and emotional states. 'Sublimity' is so called because it is the most exalted kind of worldly good" [1], and it is from here that the individual who has set out on the path, is lifted from the status of an ordinary person to that of an advanced one.

There is already a good deal of psychological insight in that which is called 'the connecting path'; as a matter of fact, to deal with the Buddhist path from any other point of view than a psycholocial one is bound to make it unintelligible. It is a recognized fact that 'warmer' feelings have a wide range of effects upon the ideas, attitudes and habits of the individual and above all serve to facilitate all sorts of learning processes. Thereby they provide a solid basis for further goal-directed activity. The 'colder' feelings of anger and hatred are definitely associated with a frustration of the impulse towards a goal and they block any on-going activity so that the individual is thrown back and has to start all over again. 'Acceptance' is a further step in the direction of the goal, although it is not yet an intimately felt experience which evolves out of the 'sublimity' stage of the 'connecting path', and only happens on the 'path of seeing'.

It is by the 'path of seeing' that one experiences no-thing-ness directly and it is its vision that releases a series of psychological processes. This no-thing-ness, which can be known by experiencing it, has been given different qualifications by the various Buddhist schools of thought in their attempt to convey its meaning to those who would like to have the experience. In so doing they all agree that this can be done only negatively; one can tell what it is not; but one cannot tell what it is. Actually, one cannot even say what it is not, because this might suggest that even after all determinate qualifications have been negated, something determinate is left. Not to be this or that is, as most Buddhists would assert, a sort of half-hearted negation which comes dangerously close to a clandestine reintroduction of ontology into Buddhism. That such an interpretation of no-thing-ness has happened is shown by the writings of Jo-nang-pa Dol-po Shes-rab rgyal-mtshan (1292-1361 A.D.) and his successors [2]. While this interpretation has been accepted by the later bKa'-brgyud-pas and some of the Sa-skya-pas, such as Shākya

---

[1] *SLNzh* 12ab.

[2] See the valuable analysis by D. S. Ruegg, *The Jo naṅ pas: A School of*

mchog-ldan (1428-1507 A.D.), generally it has been rejected by the dGe-lugs-pas. (The rNying-ma-pas also did not favour this interpretation, but since their philosophy shows individual traits no generalization is possible.) Because of the difficulty of conceptualizing that which can be known only by direct experience, although the concept must enter in any discussions, I have rendered the technical term *śūnyatā* (Tibetan: *stong-pa-nyid*) by 'no-thing-ness' and hyphenated the word so as to point to its being *no thing* and hence *nothing* from our ordinary mode of thinking which moves in terms of things. The attempts to convey something of its significance are as varied as the various schools of thought in Buddhism. For the Prāsangikas no-thing-ness is the non-existence of a self and of a thing except for the christening ceremony which is not the use of the name for the thing or self at all, but merely the way in which we give it a use. The Svātantrikas were divided into the Yogācāra-Mādhyamika-Svātantrikas (starting from the phenomenalistic-mentalistic interpretation of the Vijñānavādins disclaiming the existence of objects external to the observer) and the Sautrāntika-Mādhyamika-Svātantrikas (basing themselves on the critical realism of the Sautrāntikas who had criticized the naive realism of the Vaibhāṣikas). The former declared that a Śrāvaka realizes the 'subtle' non-existence of a self, the Pratyekabuddha the 'coarse' non-existence of the things other than the self, and the Bodhisattvas or Mahāyānists the non-existence of a self and of things as being something existing in truth. The latter declared that Śrāvakas and Pratyekabuddhas both realize the subtle nature of a self (and since they accepted things as existing apart from their being experienced, though not as true existents, Mahāyānists followed the general Svātantrika doctrine). According to the Vijñānavādins both Śrāvakas and Pratyekabuddhas realize the subtle non-existence of the self, while Mahāyānists realize the non-existence of things apart from their being experienced [1].

The distinction between a 'coarse' and 'subtle' non-existence of a self or of a thing is a carry-over from the distinction into a 'coarse' and 'subtle' idea of the existence of a self or a thing. In order to account for

---

Buddhist Ontologists According to the Grub mtha' šel gyi me lon (JAOS, vol. 83, no. 1, Jan.-March, 1963, pp. 73-91).

[1] *Tskhp* VII 1, 51b seq. The interpretation of no-thing-ness by Shin-ichi Risamatu, *The Characteristics of Oriental Nothingness* (in *Philosophical Studies of Japan*· Compiled by Japanese National Commission for Unesco. Japan Society for the Promotion of Science, Tokyo, 1960, vol. II, pp. 66 seq.) brings several aspects, which are clearly separated in the Tibetan tradition, together.

the unity of a mind (or a self) two great groups of theories have been developed, namely, Centre-Theories and Non-centre-Theories. According to C.D. Broad, "By a centre-theory I mean a theory which ascribes the unity of the mind to the fact that there is a certain particular existent – a Centre – which stands in a common asymmetrical relation to all the mental events which would be said to be states of a certain mind, and does not stand in this relation to any mental events which would not be said to be states of this mind. By a non-centre theory I mean one which denies the existence of any such particular Centre, and ascribes the unity of the mind to the fact that certain mental events are directly inter-related in certain characteristic ways, and that other mental events are not related to these in the peculiar way in which these are related to each other "[1].

Now it is obvious that Buddhism has always been favouring a non-centre theory. However, since Buddhism, did not develop in a vacuum but was confronted by other philosophical systems, its critique of these other theories regarding the unity of the mind was based on the subdivision of centre theories into Pure Ego theories and theories which do not assume a Pure Ego. Here, too, I quote C.D. Broad, as he gives the most lucid account of the possible divisions: "By a Pure Ego I understand a particular existent which is of a different kind from any event; it owns various events, but it is not itself an event. No doubt the commonest form of the Centre theory has involved a Pure Ego. But it seems conceivable that this unity of the mind might be due to the existence of a Centre, and yet that this centre might itself be an event "[2]. Such a central-event theory is "a kind of half-way between Pure Ego theories and Non-Centre theories of the mind. They resemble Pure Ego theories in the fact that the unity of the total mental state at any moment depends on a common relation in which all its differentiations stand to a common Centre. They resemble Non-Centre theories in the fact that this Centre is itself an event and not a peculiar kind of existent substantive; it is of the same nature as the events which it unifies "[3].

This distinction is at the bottom of the Buddhist differentiation into a 'coarse' and a 'subtle' theory about the self. The 'coarse' one is the assumption of a Pure Ego or the belief in a centre as being different from

---

[1] C.D. Broad, *The Mind and Its Place in Nature*. London, Routledge & Kegan Paul Ltd. (Sixth Impression), p. 558.

[2] *Ibid.*

[3] *Ibid.*, p. 566.

the events which it unites, while the 'subtle' one is the belief in such a centre as being an event of a 'self-sufficient substance', as this event is termed in the original texts. This latter belief was held by the Vātsīputrīyas, who were a sub-division of the Sarvāstivādins out of whom the Vaibhāṣikas developed. Although they believed in a centre they were still counted as Buddhists because they, too, rejected a Pure Ego or Ātman theory. Moreover, their conception of the centre as an event did not contradict the general Buddhist conception of the transitoriness of everything determinate.

The 'coarse' non-existence of things is their non-existence apart from their being experienced, which was the thesis of the Vijñānavādins who, of course, did not call this idea a 'coarse' one. The 'subtle' one is the non-existence of things in truth, as professed by the Prāsangikas and Svātantrikas.

Regardless of whatever meaning may be given to no-thing-ness, its immediate experience on the 'path of seeing' initiates the elimination of emotionally upsetting factors which in Mahāyāna is supplemented by the elimination of intellectually-cognitively disturbing ones as well. The 'path of seeing' is a complex psychological process and its beginning is marked by a 'composure awareness' which is concentrated on no-thing-ness. This clearly shows that the 'path' in Buddhism as a cognitive process has an intentional structure, no-thing-ness being the intentional object of the knowing agent who in the act of knowing achieves cognitive union with this object. This composure awareness brings about the elimination of the disturbing factors by means of its 'obstacle-removing' phase which is followed by a 'free-moving' one in which the elimination has been effected. Both phases are accompanied by a psychological process which cannot be determined as either obstacle-removing or freemoving. It is, however, this process which guarantees its continuity by letting the 'composure awareness' pass into its subsequent 'continual awareness' which, in turn, is followed by a phase which is neither composure nor continual and thereby merges into the 'path of attending to the seen'. This latter 'path' is as complex a process as the 'path of seeing'. In its last phase it merges into the 'path of no more learning' by which the goal has been attained.

The emotivity which is eliminated by the obstacle-removing phase and which is no longer a danger when the free-moving phase has been reached (the first phase is likened to the catching of a thief and the second one to throwing him out of the house and locking the door) bears on the four truths in Buddhism which, by seeing no-thing-ness, can be accepted whole-heartedly. These four truths are those of misery and of the origin of misery (which are emotively toned responses and karmic actions) and their countering truths of the end of all misery and the way to it. Each pair stands in the relation of cause and effect, but the order has been reversed for a special reason. Unless the fact is brought home to us that all that to which we are accustomed and take for granted is unsatisfactory, we will never feel called upon to do something in order to end this state of affairs. The Fifth Dalai Lama illustrates the four truths as follows: "When one stands in a dry place and it should happen that one's body, clothes and other belongings get drenched by water and one shivers with cold, this is the truth of misery. The certainty that this water has come from a certain place, when one has investigated its approach, is the truth of the origin of misery. Ridding oneself of the feeling of cold is the truth of the end of misery. The work of diverting the flow of the water, as a means of getting rid of the feeling of cold, is the truth of the path (to the end of misery) [1]".

The whole-hearted acceptance of these truths eliminates the emotively toned responses to that which they sum up. These responses comprise both feeling-emotional and intellectual-emotional ones such as passion and hatred, feeling of superiority and preconceived ideas about that which we encounter. Through the elimination of these emotional responses the 'acceptance' of the truths becomes a directly felt 'cognition'. This is indicated by the statement that the 'acceptance' of the truths happens on the obstacle-removing path and their 'cognition' on the free-moving one [2].

There is a marked difference between the first phase or 'composure awareness' of the 'path of seeing' and its subsequent one or 'continual awareness'. The former is an immediate apprehension of no-thing-ness, while the latter is a judgment of perception. However, this difference holds only for the 'learner' who still has to travel the 'path of attending to the seen' and 'the path of no more learning'. For him who is on the Buddha level from where he sees reality as it is, both phases, composure awareness and continual awareness, are of the same nature. This means that the vividness of the experience of seeing is kept alive throughout. Only when this happens should one speak of the indivisibility of no-thing-ness and apparitionalness. Things are nothing in themselves, but this does not imply that there is nothing. Furthermore, for the Prāsan-

[1] *Zhl* 36b seq.

[2] Inasmuch as there are Four Truths which equally apply to the lower world of sensuality and the higher worlds of pure form and formlessness, there are eight acceptances and eight cognitions.

gikas, judgment of perception is a valid cognition; not so for the Svātantrikas who relegate all such judgments to the realm of an erring mind.

The intellectual fog which has to be eliminated by a Mahāyānist in addition to that of emotivity and wishfulness, relates to the subject-object mode of thinking which prevents us from apprehending things directly as they are in and for themselves, because this mode of thinking is always mixed up with appetance and with purposefulness. Things or persons, here, are not ends in themselves, but are there for a purpose, for use (and misuse) for a definite (and mostly absurd) end. In this subject-object dichotomy the subject and object are bound together in such a way that the one cannot be without the other. Hence whatever I experience resides in the whole of this subject-object dichotomy, never only in one term. Ordinarily we are always involved in the objects of our thoughts and in the projects which relate to how we are going to be. These projects are never without alternatives. There is that which arouses emotively toned responses directly or indirectly. For this reason the objective pole of this subject-object structure is divided into two alternatives, one of which brings about an emotional situation immediately and one which remedies it. In order to go beyond the subject-object dichotomy and to become free from the involvements in one's projects one first has to bring the biased project clearly before one's eyes or, in psychological terms and as detailed by C.G. Jung in his many writings, to tackle the disturbing emotional situation and, in its cognition for what it is, to be freed from the hold it has over us. This, in most cases, first means a resort to the antidote of the existing emotional situation. The antidote, however, if not recognized for what it is, may become an emotional situation as fatal as the one it attempts to combat. Therefore both aspects of the objective pole have to be recognized in their relation to each other. In becoming aware of our projects with their alternatives we are also aware of ourselves as projecting. That is, we can distinguish between our projects and our conceiving and judging them. The subjective pole is therefore subdivided also into two projecting modes, the one concretizing and substantializing, the other conceptualizing and abstracting.

The elimination of wishfulness and emotivity as well as that of intellectual fog is effected by the 'path of seeing' and the 'path of attending to the seen'. By means of the former those disturbing elements are removed which are rather extraneous inasmuch as they are those to which we have been 'conditioned' by our up-bringing, while by the latter those which are co-emergent with the developing subject-object dichotomy are abolished. With the complete removal of everything preventing the immediate apprehension of reality and of keeping its vivid experience alive, be this emotional or intellectual, the 'path of no more learning' has been reached and the goal attained.

The 'path' in Buddhism is essentially the account of man's growth, one important feature of which is the integration of the personality. The path depends on the concept which the individual has of himself, and so does the development of character, of religious, moral and social values, because that which a person thinks of himself cannot fail to affect his level of aspiration and his interaction with others at every turn. This goal-consciousness must be reinforced by a constantly growing appreciation of values in terms of which the worth-whileness of certain experiences and the superficial character of others can be estimated. This happens by developing the capacity to 'see' from a point of view which is removed from all presuppositions. This view realizes that things are not entities fixed once for all, that there is not an essence through which something is what it is; and in this realization it also abolishes the last trace of the belief in something as existing in truth. As Tsong-kha-pa declares: "In order to abolish the tendency to believe in something as existing in truth, which is the root of Saṃsāra, not only must one intuit no-thing-ness by which one understands that the psycho-physical constituents of our being have no being of their own, there also must be present the intellectual acumen which understands this non-existence of an essence, in order to cut the fetters of emotional responses and karmic actions that tie us to Saṃsāra" [1].

Thus, the 'path' leads to self-realization, to Buddhahood as the highest and most sublime idea of man (not an ideal because ideals may break), and the vision of no-thing-ness, the 'middle view', takes the sting out of Saṃsāra.

---

[1] *Tskhp* VII 1, 48a. At the same place Tsong-kha-pa declares that the view which apprehends the fact that there is no self and that no ontological status can be assigned to anything, is the same for the Sūtras and Tantras. This means that the objective reference is the same throughout the two aspects of Mahāyāna: Pāramitāyāna and Mantrayāna.

CHAPTER FIVE

PĀRAMITĀYĀNA AND MANTRAYĀNA

Mahāyāna, the 'Great Spiritual Course', is known as the 'spiritual course of Bodhisattvas' in order to distinguish it from the 'Lesser Course' or Hīnayāna with the two divisions, Śrāvakayāna and Pratyekabuddhayāna, both of which are recognized by Mahāyāna as preliminary steps. Śrāvakayāna is the spiritual course of those who 'listen' to the discourses of religious masters, have to be told everything regarding what to do and what not to do, and are unable to find their way and attain their goal without that continuous guidance upon which they thoroughly depend. In the course of human development the Śrāvaka belongs to the infancy stage. Pratyekabuddhayāna is the course of the self-reliant persons who by their own power want to go their way and reach their goal. They may be persons of the lone-wolf type, men of the common herd, or selective persons who carefully choose their company. The common characteristic of Śrāvakas and Pratyekabuddhas is their self-centredness which is only mitigated by the circumstance that in following a certain discipline they may become living examples of how to pursue the aim of self-development and in this way have a mediate effect on society.

The spiritual course of the Bodhisattvas or of those who belong to the superior type of man in the triple classification of mankind and who have realized that the idea of man is never an image of fulfilment but merely a stimulus to his desire to rise above himself, comprises two courses which closely intermingle and, indeed, are complementary to each other, Pāramitāyāna and Mantrayāna.

Pāramitāyāna, as its name implies, emphasizes the practice of the 'perfections' of liberality, ethics and manners, patience, strenuousness, meditative concentration, and intelligence as the function which apprehends no-thing-ness. The former five are subsumed under 'fitness of action' or the moral frame within which the sixth, intelligence, operates as a discriminative and appreciative function. Precisely because of its capacity to intuit reality as it is and to appreciate it by separating it from all its adumbrations due to wishfulness and uncritical thinking, it is a truly transcending function and leads man out of bondage to freedom as an active and dynamic way of being. This is realized by scaling the ten spiritual levels which commence when the path of 'seeing reality or no-thing-ness' opens, and continues by the path of 'attending to the seen' to the path of 'no more learning' or goal-attainment. It is on these levels that the perfections can express themselves properly and do not degenerate into sentimentalities and affectations. Other, though less known, names for this aspect of Mahāyāna Buddhism are Lakṣaṇayāna (course of philosophical investigation) and Hetuyāna (course of spiritual training in which attention is centred on the ultimate cognitive norm in human experience).

Mantrayāna (its full name is Guhya-mantra-phala-vajra-yāna) is variously called Guhyamantrayāna, Phalayāna, Upāyayāna, and Vajrayāna. The term Vajrayāna has become the common name for this aspect of Mahāyāna Buddhism which has been misrepresented grossly by writers of different professions, mostly for two reasons. The first is plain ignorance. The Vajrayāna texts deal with inner experiences and their language is highly symbolical. These symbols must be understood as symbols for the peculiar kind of experience which brought forth the peculiar verbal response, not for things which adequately (and even exhaustively) can be referred to by the literal language of everyday life. The symbols of Vajrayāna do not stand literally for anything, they are meant as a help "to lead people to, and finally to evoke within them, certain *experiences* which those who have had them consider to be the most worth-while of all experiences available to human beings" [1]. In brief, the language of Vajrayāna is mystical and although it has an essentially material element in it, its intention is *never* material. The second reason for gross misrepresentation is that writers about Vajrayāna have already made up their minds about the nature of Buddhism. This attitude has its root in the peculiar outlook that developed in the West after the Middle Ages. There was, here, a progressive emphasis upon knowledge which was born from the desire to achieve control over nature together with a possible transformation of cultural patterns. Such a knowledge-norm does not take kindly to accepting and appreciating different cultural forms or different premises of thought in their own right. It automatically will fit any

---

[1] John Hospers, *Introduction to Philosophical Analysis*. London, Routledge & Kegan Paul Ltd. 1956, p. 374.

factual information about something alien to it into its preconceived schemata. As a matter of fact, that which is to be considered as factual or 'objective' (or whatever revised version of this now threadbare abstraction may be brought forward) is already a selection from the vast amount of data that eventually will be made to suit the existing pattern. Everything else is pushed into the background or dismissed as not being relevant; otherwise it remains unintelligible why patently absurd theories should be perpetuated [1].

The long, though unwieldy, term Guhya-mantra-phala-vajra-yāna can be translated as 'a course grounded in the ultimate structure of the noetic as taking shape in active Buddhahood, and which is the crowning result of a process of transformation that remains hidden to the ordinary observer'. It points to every feature peculiar to this aspect of Mahāyāna. Its meaning has been given by Tsong-kha-pa as follows [2]:

"Since it is hidden and concealed and not an object for those who are not fit for it, it is 'secret' (*gsang-ba, guhya*).

"The etymology of *mantra* is *man* 'mentation' and *tra* 'protection', as laid down in the *Guhyasamājatantra* (p. 156) [3]:

Mentation which proceeds
Through senses and sense-objects
Is named *manas;*
Protection is meant by *tra*
That which Liberation from wordliness is said to be
Consists of commitments and restraints;
To guard them with existential
Norms is said to be the Mantra-conduct.

"Another explanation is that *man* refers to the awareness of reality as it is and *tra* to compassion protecting sentient beings.

---

[1] Closely connected with this peculiar outlook is the traditional religious background of the West. It took over from the Semitic conception the story of the Fall of Man and this Biblical tale underlies openly or covertly all accounts about the history of the development of Buddhist thought. Inasmuch as erotic imagery is taboo in the Western traditional religion, this local belief is nevertheless made the basis for judging cultural patterns that have a different premise and can be understood only from grasping them in their own right. Tantrism puts no premium or sanction on sexual licence. Its moral code is about the strictest that can be demanded.

[2] *Tskhp* III 12a seqq.

[3] See also *Tskhp* VI 4, 10a.

"'Course' (*theg-pa, yāna*) is both goal-attainment or result, and goal-approach or causal situation, and since there is goal-directed movement, one speaks of a 'course'.

"'Result' (*'bras-bu, phala*) refers to the four purities of place, being, wealth, and action, *i.e.*, the citadel of Buddhahood, the Buddha-norms (of cognition and communication), the Buddha-riches, and the Buddha-activities. When in anticipation of this goal one imagines oneself now as being engaged in the purification of the without and within by sacred utensils in the midst of gods (and goddesses) in a divine palatial mansion, one speaks of a Phalayāna (a course which anticipates the goal), because one proceeds by a meditation which anticipates the result. Thus it is stated in the *Bla-med-kyi rgyud-don-la 'jug-pa:* 'Result –, because one proceeds by way of the purities of existence, wealth, place, and action'.

"The *Vimalaprabhā* states: 'Vajra means sublime indivisibility and indestructibility, and since this is (the nature of) the course, one speaks of Vajraship'. This is to say that Vajrayāna is the indivisibility of cause or Pāramitā method and effect or Mantra method. – According to the *dBang mdor bstan:*

> Awareness of no-thing-ness is the cause;
> To feel unchanging bliss is the effect.
> The indivisibility of no-thing-ness
> And bliss is known as the enlightenment of mind.

"Here the indivisibility of awareness which directly intuits no-thingness and the unchanging, supreme bliss is conceived as consisting of the two phenomena of goal-approach and goal-attainment. Such an interpretation of Vajrayāna, however, applies to the Anuttarayogatantras, not to the three lower Tantras, because, if this unchanging, supreme bliss has to be effected by meditative practices preceding and including inspection, since it settles after the bliss-no-thing-ness concentration has been realized, these causal factors are not present in their entirety in the lower Tantras. Therefore, while this is correct for the general idea of Vajrayāna, it is not so for the distinction in a causal situation course or in one anticipating the goal. For this reason the explanation of the *sNyim-pa'i me-tog* will have to be added: 'The essence of Mahāyāna is the six perfections; their essence is fitness of action and intelligence of which the essence or one-valueness is the enlightenment-mind. Since this it the Vajrasattva-concentration it is Vajra, and being both Vajra and a spiritual course, one speaks of Vajrayāna. And this is the meaning of

Mantrayoga'. Thus Vajrayāna is synonymous with Vajrasattva-yoga which effects the indivisible union of fitness of action and intelligence. In it there are the two phases of a path and a goal.

"'Upāyayāna' (course of methods) means that the methods stressed in this course are superior to those of the Pāramitāyāna. As stated in the *mTha' gnyis sel-ba*: 'Because of indivisibility, the goal being the path, superiority of methods and utter secrecy, one speaks of Vajrayāna, Phalayāna, Upāyayāna, and Guyha(mantra)yāna respectively'".

This authoritative interpretation of the meaning of Pāramitāyāna and Mantrayāna needs only a few words by way of comment. Mantrayāna certainly is a hidden and secret lore, not because something that is offensive has to be concealed, but because it is nothing tangibly concrete that one can display. It is something which relates to that which is most intimate: the refinement of the personality, the cultivation of human values, the liberation of man from his bondage to things and, above all, from the mistaken and debasing idea that he himself is a thing, a narrowly circumscribed entity in a vast array of impersonal and inhuman things. Certainly, a discipline which aims at preventing life from becoming a mere vegetative function and at rescuing man from being lost in an all-devouring, spiritless, unspirited, and inhuman mass, is of no value to him whose only desire is to be led in such a way that he believes he is a leader. It is with regard to such people that Mantrayāna has to be kept hidden and must never be divulged. A person who has not yet become fit and mature through having practised all that which is common to both Sūtras and Tantras by following the graded path of the 'three types of man' – 'the person who is not a suitable receptacle for instruction', as the texts repeatedly refer to him – is unable to understand its significance and by his lack of understanding is merely courting disaster. He will at once try to turn it into something which it never can be. Enmeshed in his superstitions and goaded on by rash conclusions he will discount new and divergent insights as already long familiar, and he will level down the exceptional to the average (if not the below-average). For he hates to be forced to stand on his own feet; after all it is so much easier and reassuring to find oneself supported by a prevailing opinion, even if it should be a most absurd one.

Every developmental process is something that occurs in the secret depths of man's being and that has to be guarded carefully against and protected from all that might interfere with it. This is done by remaining aware of what is real. Therefore at every phase the contemplation of no-thing-ness is an inevitable accompaniment. Once this awareness is lost man glides off into uncertainty and becomes susceptible of error. Although in Buddhism error never implies culpability, it must be overcome because it is a straying away from an initial vividness and richness of experience into a bewildering state of disintegration and dead concepts. Such a necessary protection is offered by the *mantra* which, as a rule, is either decried as unintelligible gibberish or believed to possess occult powers, all of which merely serves to mystify the issue. The *mantra*, like the visualized images of gods and goddesses, is a symbol which, precisely because it has no assigned connotation as has the literal sign we use in propositions, is capable of being understood in more significant ways, so that its meanings are frought with vital and sentient experience. The *mantra* opens a new avenue of thought which becomes truer to itself than does any other type of thinking which has found its limit in de-vitalized symbols or signs that can be used to signify anything without themselves being significant.

Being a course (*yāna*) of transformation and transfiguration in which the goal determines the course, Mantrayāna demands a different kind of thought, which in the very act of thinking transforms *me* and in so doing brings *me* nearer to *myself*. This is not so much an achievement which, once it has been performed, can be labelled and shelved somewhere, because as a new determinate and narrowly circumscribed state it would be as much a fetter as was the previous one. Rather, it remains a task which opens our eyes to new horizons. In other words, the goal is the project of myself as I am going to be when all bias due to direct and indirect indoctrination is abolished, and since our projects are not isolated events locked up inside a mind, they refer to a whole world and its ordering. The goal, commonly referred to as Buddhahood, is never a fixed determinate essence; it is a whole world-view. There is the 'citadel of Buddhahood' or the divine mansion which is not empty but lived in by 'bodies' or more precisely by body-minds, which give this world its divine status by reaching out to it by means of existentials, the norms of spirituality, communication, and authentic being in the world. There is the richness of communication as an act of worship and lastly an enactment of Buddhahood, the transformation and transfiguration of oneself and of the world in producing a new pattern that is more promising and more satisfying. Since one acts here in support of a goal as yet unrealized, this discipline is aptly called the course which makes the goal its base. This does not exclude its 'cause', the Pāramitāyāna, which lays the foundation for an intellectual and spiritual maturation. This enables man to acquire the values, ideals, and principles with which he can create for himself those future forms of understanding which will impart meaning to his life through a constantly growing appreciation in terms of which he can estimate the worth-whileness of certain things and acts and the futility of others.

The indivisibility of cause and effect is one of the many meanings of *vajra*. In this sense Vajrayāna is synonymous with Mantrayāna and is the name for a technique or course of action which is controlled by the goal, the 'result' towards which the act is directed. In other words, the end controls the means, but the action is here and now, although the goal to be reached is still at some 'place', the citadel of Buddhahood which in the pure Buddha-sphere is the Akaniṣṭha-heaven and in the human-divine sphere the palatial mansion of the *maṇḍala*, both of which are as yet undetermined in ordinary place and time. This is not purposive in the ordinary sense of the word, it is an integrative process of a higher order. It leads to the second meaning of *vajra* and indicates the blending of action and insight. In theory, we may separate awareness from action, but as phases of our being they are closely interdependent. The more I understand myself as being a fixed entity the more degraded my actions become; and, conversely, the less self-centred I become the less biased are my actions and relations with others. The unificatory process is named Vajrasattva-yoga. In Buddhism, *yoga* never means to be swallowed up by an Absolute, nor does it imply anything which Occidental faddism fancies it to be; it always means the union of 'fitness of action' and 'intelligence'. In this process certain norms are revealed, which are always active and dynamic. They have become known by their Indian names, Dharmakāya, Sambhogakāya, and Nirmāṇakāya, but never have been understood properly, within the framework of traditional Western semantics, because of the essentialist premises of Western philosophies. Essence is that which marks a thing off and separates it from other entities of a different kind. From such a point of view all of man's actions spring from that which is considered to be his intrinsic nature. Its fallacy is that it makes us overlook man's relational being; the actual person always lives *in* a world *with* others. And, in human life, essence tells man that he is already what he can be, so there is no need to set out on a path of spiritual development.

Seen as existential norms these three patterns reveal their significance. Dharmakāya indicates the intentional structure of the noetic in man. It is the merit of Buddhism that it has always recognized this feature of awareness: I cannot know without knowing something, just as I cannot do without doing something. But in ordinary knowledge whatever

I know is overshadowed by beliefs, presuppositions, likes and dislikes. However, the more I succeed in removing myself from self-centred concerns and situations and free myself from all bias, the more I am enabled to apprehend things as they are. This happens in disciplined philosophical enquiry through which one gradually approaches no-thingness and indeterminacy, from the vantage point of which one can achieve a view of reality without internal warping. This cognitive indeterminacy which underlies the whole noetic enterprise of man is richer in contents and broader in its horizons than any other awareness because it is an unrestricted perspective from which nothing is screened or excluded. If anything can be predicated about it, it is pure potency which, when actualized, enables us to see ourselves and things as we and they really are. In order to gain this capacity we have to develop our intelligence, our critical acumen, which is the main theme of the Pāramitāyāna and without which Mantrayāna is impossible. But all the information we receive through such sustained analysis is not merely for the sake of pure awareness or contemplation, but in order that we may act. Every insight is barren if it does not find expression in action, and every action is futile if it is not supported by sound insight. Only when we succeed in understanding ourselves, our projects and our world from a point of view which is no point of view, will a sound direction of human action be possible, because it is no longer subordinated to petty, self-centred concerns. This active mode of being is realized through the two operational patterns or norms, the Sambhogakāya and the Nirmāṇakāya, both of which have their *raison d'être* in the cognitive-spiritual mode. Strictly speaking, only the Nirmāṇakāya is perceptible, although it would be wrong to assume that it is of a physical nature. As a matter of fact, as ordinary beings we are unable to discern whether somebody embodies the Nirmāṇakāya or not. Only at some later time, after centuries and generations may we come to realize that this person or that has been that which we would term the Nirmāṇakāya. This gives the clue to an understanding of this technical term which is left untranslated in works dealing with Buddhism. Nirmāṇakāya signifies being in the world, not so much as a being among things and artifacts, but as an active being in relation to a vast field of surrounding entities which are equally vibrating with life, all of them ordered in a world structure. As an active mode of being Nirmāṇakāya is the implementation of man's whole being, the ordering of his world in the light of his ultimate possibilities.

In our everyday life we understand others, for the most part, from what they do, the functions they perform, and this appears to be a static and impersonal order. Anyone may perform this function or that. The main thing is that business goes on. There is little scope for the Nirmāṇakāya, because that would be something exceptional, and the exceptional is at once levelled down to the average. However, the ordering of one's life and of the world in which one lives is certainly not an impersonal or depersonalized act. Man is never alone, but always reaches out to others. He does this through communication. Usually this happens in the verbosity of everyday chatter. The more words that are uttered the more there seems to have been said, and therefore some modern philosophers think that a proper manipulation of linguistic symbols will solve all problems of being. Just as a world of things cannot give meaning to man's being *in* the world, the verbose discourse indulged in by various groups is unable to clarify man's being *with* others. Universal concepts and ready-made judgments are utterly inadequate. Real being with others must spring up on the spur of the moment and arouse us to our possibilities. That which does so is the Sambhogakāya. Grounded in unrestricted and unbiased cognition it can establish contact with others and stir them to authentic action.

The union of insight and action, of unlimited cognition and its active framework of communication *with* others *in* a world order, is referred to by the symbol of Vajrasattva: "*Vajra* is the Dharmakāyic awareness in which three types of enlightenment enter indivisibly from ultimateness, and *Sattva* is the apprehendable form pattern deriving from it" [1]. The attempt to effect this integration of thought and action is termed Vajrasattvayoga, which is synonymous with Vajrayāna.

There is yet another meaning to Vajrasattva, which is the central theme of the highest form of Mantrayāna, the Anuttarayogatantra or 'the continuity of the unificatory process which is unsurpassed'. This truly inward event is represented symbolically by two human bodies in intimate embrace. This is so because the human body is the easiest form in which we can understand that which is most important to us, and the embrace is the most intimate connection that can exist between two different persons. This seemingly sexual symbolism has shocked many an observer who merely read his own pre-occupation with sex into the symbol representation and completely failed to grasp the premises from which this symbolism sprang. L. A. Reid aptly remarks: "There is mythic thinking here, and it is necessary. It is not the end or the last word, but only one way in which we physically bodied creatures can live intensely

---

[1] *Tskhp* I 10, 2ab.

our spiritual life. The same is true of sexual love when it is fully human. The lover desires physical contact, almost identification and assimilation of the beloved, which is one unique way in which a person can achieve closest spiritual unity with another. The language of poetry and religion which expresses these things is mystic language. It has an essentially material element in it, but its intention is not finally material or it would be mere idolatry or sensuality. In our embodied experience the two aspects are so interfused that the language of space and time and of actions therein is the language of the spirit as embodied" [1]. Certainly, such symbol language and representation is more effective than to say abstractly that *Vajra* is the symbol for the noetic which is present as an indeterminate relational form, grounded in the knowing agent, and that *Sattva* is determinate and has apparently its own ground, and that this duality, which we encounter as the subject-object division, is overcome when the indeterminate relational form is terminated or filled by the object and thus becomes determinate. It is cold comfort to speak of Vajrasattva as the symbol of noetic identity, where identity is formal, not existential; and this becomes still more uncomfortable when we consider it merely from a cognitive-intellectual aspect, because we have tended to separate feeling from knowing and to consider them as incompatible. In Buddhism, knowing has a connotation of bliss, while unknowing is suffering. This bliss reaches its highest pitch when knowledge becomes free, when nothing restricts the range of its possible terms. Cognition is thus commensurate with ecstasy. This experience is technically known as the 'indivisibility of bliss and no-thing-ness' which Tsong-kha-pa defines as follows: "When the subjective pole or the noetic, which has become its existentially inherent bliss, understands the objective pole or no-thing-ness without internal warping, this union of subject and object is the indivisible unity of bliss and no-thing-ness" [2].

The recognition of existential categories as dynamic ways of being centres attention on how man acts rather than on what he is. The Sūtras, on which the Pāramitāyāna bases its teaching, give us a disciplined analysis of man's cognitive capacity, but they do not, or at least not with unmistakable clarity and distinctness, study the active modes by which this power realizes itself in ordering the world *in* which we live *with* others. Since we cannot live well with others unless we have first de-

---

[1] *Ways of Knowledge and Experience*, p. 147.
[2] *Tskhp* VII 1, 55b.

veloped a decisive insight into our nature and our role in establishing a world order, the Sūtras are a preliminary step in this direction as they concentrate on the development of the cognitive capacity which, when brought to utmost clarity, enables man to set out on the Mahāyāna path. Thus Mantrayāna and Pāramitāyāna, contrary to the opinion of certain scholars, are not two different and incompatible aspects of Buddhism, but are complementary to each other because the one concentrates on the development of an unbiased outlook and an unrestricted perspective, the other on the implementation of the cognitive norm through operational ones in authentic being with others and for others in a world that has been ordered in the light of man's ultimate and existential norms. This complementary character of Mantrayāna and Pāramitāyāna is clearly evident from Tsong-kha-pa's and other Tibetan sages' writings. Tsong-kha-pa's words are [1]:

"Buddhahood, which fulfils the needs of others by manifesting itself to them, does not do so through the cognitive norm, the Dharmakāya, but through the two operational ones, the Sambhogakāya and Nirmāṇakāya. In this respect it is the philosophical conviction of all Mahāyānists that the realization of the cognitive norm through intelligent appreciative discrimination which intuitively apprehends the profound nature (or no-thing-ness) of all that is, that the realization of the two operational norms comes through unbounded activity, and that insight and action must for ever work together because they are unable to effect anything if they are divorced from each other. Intelligence which apprehends the profound nature of all that is, is the same in Mantrayāna as it is in the two lower courses (Hīnayāna and Pāramitāyāna), because without understanding existentiality it is impossible to cross the ocean of Saṃsāra by exhausting our emotional reactions. Therefore, the special and prominent feature of the Mahāyāna path is the instrumentality of the two operational norms which manifest themselves to the prepared and serve as a protective guidance to sentient beings as long as Saṃsāra lasts. Although the followers of the Pāramitāyāna attend to an inner course that corresponds to the ultimate cognitive norm by conceiving the nature of all that is as beyond the judgments of reason and as not existing in truth, they have no such course as the one of Mantrayāna which corresponds to the richness of operational modes. Therefore, because there is a great difference in the main feature of the path, the realization of operational norms for the sake of others, there is the division into two courses. While

---

[1] *Ibid.*, III 15b.

the division into Hīnayāna and Mahāyāna is due to the means employed and not because of a difference in the nature of intelligence through which no-thing-ness is apprehended, the division of the Mahāyāna into Pāramitāyāna and Mantrayāna also is not due to a difference in the discriminative acumen which understands the profound nature of all that is, but because of the techniques employed. The differentiating quality is the realization of operational norms, and the transfigurational technique which effects the realization of these norms is superior to all other techniques used in the other courses".

From this it follows that the combination of Pāramitāyāna and Mantrayāna is more effective than any course pursued alone, although each course has its goal-achievement. This, too, has been stated by Tsong-kha-pa [1]:

"It has been said that one is liberated from Saṃsāra when one knows properly both the Mantrayāna and Pāramitāyāna methods. Common to both is the idea that, failing to understand the nature of mind as not existing as a self, through the power of believing it to be a self all other emotional upsets are generated, and through them, in turn, karmic actions are performed, and because of these actions one roams about in Saṃsāra. Specific to the Anuttarayogatantra is the idea that motivity, which spreads from an indestructible creativity centre in the region of the heart as a focal point of experience, initiates emotively toned responses by which karmic actions are performed. If one does not know how this process comes into existence, and finally recedes gradually into this centre, one is fettered in Saṃsāra. This means that, when regarding the common process of birth and death one has realized the necessity of finding that point of view which one intuitively apprehends the non-existence of a self, as explained by the Mādhyamika philosophy, one will become utterly convinced about the efficacy of this view which makes the round of birth and death ineffective. It also means that in regard to the specific process of birth and death one realizes the necessity of knowing the specific means to make ineffective motility, which initiates emotively toned responses. This latter method, however, is not necessary for merely becoming liberated from Saṃsāra, because Śrāvakas and Pratyekabuddhas also find deliverance from Saṃsāra, although they do not resort to this special method of Mantrayāna. It is (commonly) claimed that it is not enough to eliminate overt emotional responses which cause one to roam about in Saṃsāra, but that all their latent potentialities

[1] *Ibid.*, VI 3 34b seq.

have to be eliminated in addition. Yet it is the claim (of Mantrayāna) that Buddhahood is found quickly, and not realized only after many aeons as it is stated in the Pāramitāyāna works. When the emotively toned responses such as passion, aversion and others which fetter beings in Saṃsāra and which in the Pāramitāyāna have been said to arise from the belief in a self, have been abolished, their power has come to an end. This is because, though they have not been shown to arise from motility, motility aids them when they have come into existence by the belief in a self as the organizatory cause. Therefore, if one does not have the discriminative acumen which apprehends the non-existence of a self, the real means to stop the organizatory power of the belief in a self which brings about Saṃsāra, one will not be able to become free from Saṃsāra, even if the generally aiding power of motility has been stopped. Hence both procedures are necessary. While the former method has the capacity to eliminate emotively toned responses completely, it does so more quickly when it combines with the latter method; hence Mantrayāna is the quick path".

Two points deserve special notice. The one is the statement that Mantrayāna is a quick method; the other is the specific terminology of this discipline which deals with the same subject matter as does the Pāramitāyāna. The language of the Sūtras, which are the basis of the Pāramitāyāna, is 'nominal' and propositional inasmuch as that which is stated can be apprehended intellectually with but incidental references to experience. What the Sūtras say can be said again quite intelligibly without, however, having any concern in that to which it pertains. The language of Mantrayāna, on the other hand, attempts to express valuable experiences, which are 'felt' knowledge rather than knowledge 'about' something. Following the distinction by L. A. Reid [1], it is important always to be aware that the language of Mantrayāna is 'embodying' language, while that of the Pāramitāyāna is predominantly 'categorizing'. And as it is not immediately necessary to experience what the Sūtras teach, they can be studied at arm's length (although they were never meant to be dealt with in such a way, to be discussed at social gatherings where 'interesting' people are inordinately puffed up with their own importance). It will readily be admitted that it will take a long, indeed, a very long time until one 'feels' what it is all about. Mantrayāna, which is always 'felt' knowledge, presupposes 'engagement' and therefore is immediate. But there lies the tremendous danger which is not realized

---

[1] *Ways of Knowledge and Experience*, pp. 114 seqq.

by those who crave for that which is labelled 'Tantrism'. Unless properly prepared by first having developed one's intellectual acumen and having gained an unrestricted perspective, which is a most gruelling process, there is no chance to realize the goal; insanity in its milder or more severe form has too often been the outcome for those who attempted a short-cut in spiritual development. While it is possible to gain an unrestricted perspective, a 'middle view', without pursuing the path of self-development, Mantrayāna is indissolubly connected with this path for which the initiatory empowerment is a necessity. This is so because the empowerment itself releases an experiental process which must be guarded by the strictest self-discipline.

Although Mantrayāna is the climax of Buddhist spiritual culture, it remains in itself a graded process. This is evident from its division into Kriyātantra, Caryātantra, Yogatantra, and Anuttarayogatantra.

The word Tantra defies any attempt at translation, because it is too complex to be rendered adequately. It denotes all that is otherwise described as the ground, the path, and the goal [1]. As the ground it is the primal source from which everything takes its life and seems to lie beyond all that is empirical and objective. It is a light by which one sees rather than that which one sees. And in this illuminating character it is the ground against which everything objective stands revealed. It has no specific traits of its own and seems to be a vast continuum out of which all specific entities are shaped. As the ground it is the self-conscious existence of the individual who through this awareness is stirred to express himself in the light of his possibilities. In so expressing himself he travels a path that is graded towards an apex. This travelling along the road of self-development is an unfolding of infinite riches, rather than a march from one point to another. Unhindered by tendencies to consider goal-achievement as a final state, the goal remains an inspiring source. Since the ground is often called the cause and the goal the effect, in between which comes the path, one is tempted to think of the causal situation as a linear succession of events. But such an idea is foreign to Mantrayāna which takes the effect for its way. There is certainly a directive behaviour, but the determination of the pattern of action is intrinsic to the process. There is no external agent acting upon a natural process as a *deus ex machina* in some mysterious ways which we are told we will never be able to understand. Although there is no causality in the traditional

---

[1] *Guhyasamājatantra*. Baroda, Oriental Institute 1931, p. 153. See also my 'Introduction' to *A New Tibetan Pantheon*. New Delhi 1961.

pragmatic sense, a genuine teleology seems to be involved, which is best called the principle of circular causation. The idea of the end or the goal determines and motivates conduct, but to have an idea of the future is a present act. Thus Tantra is both man's existence and transcendence, his beginning and end. But to state it in this way is to prejudge and to misconstrue it, for beginning and end contradict continuity, and existence introduces a static element which is not recognized in Buddhism. Here one encounters an almost insoluble difficulty. Most of our Western terms are statically explicit, while almost all Buddhist terms are dynamically suggestive. The basic idea of Tantra as continuity does not imply a survival in another form. It, rather, is a time-negating immersion in that which appears to man as a path of action continued for ever in time.

Inasmuch as man is the central theme of Buddhism, it has been realized from the very beginning that he finds himself continually in a world and in interaction with others. Since interaction is between persons who are men and women, it is only natural that male and female symbols occur throughout man's development. Development aims at integration, which essentially means unity and harmony within the individual, a harmony between wishes, thoughts, purposes and actions. The integrating process itself takes on the character of a social act because it involves interaction with others both direct and indirect, overt and symbolic. Such interaction may most easily be compared to the progressive stages in courtship. Every incipient love relationship is to a great extent a matter of the eyes. The foreplay is almost completely concentrated in the exchange of glances, which is then followed by smiles, a grasping of the hands (which in various cultures is a tacit consent to proceding towards the final stage of the love play), and physical consummation. Courtship is thus the readiest symbol to illustrate a process of integration which always means the unity between diverse factors. Just as integration is a need, so man needs a woman. But it is an important feature of this need that in all societies and under all known circumstances woman has always been regarded as something more than the mere object for satisfying a physiological urge. Woman has always been a source of inspiration, whether she has been an image in man's psyche or a concrete person in the physical world. The within and the without intermingle and it is difficult to draw a dividing line. That which is an inward drama is depicted in terms of the relationship between man and woman in the outer world as a deep and growing consummation in which the bodily and the spiritual indivisibly blend in the one life which constitutes the union of two individuals; and that which is an outward act becomes an inner stimulus to a transfigured existential unity. The four phases of courtship: exchange of glances, an appreciating and encouraging smile, a grasping of the hands, and the consummatory sexual act, symbolize the gradation of the four Tantras: Kriyā-, Caryā-, Yoga-, and Anuttarayogatantra. "Those who can identify their desire to look at the goddess of their contemplation with the path of their spiritual development are taught the Kriyātantra; those who, in addition, are able to smile at their partner, but cannot do more than this, are given the Caryātantra; those who can hold the hands of the inspiring female or desire bodily contact, but are unable to proceed further towards the consummatory act, are taught the Yogatantra; and those who not only stay with contemplation but make the desire to copulate with a real woman the path of their spiritual growth, are taught the Anuttarayogatantra "[1].

The description of a psychological process of integration in the symbol of a love relationship, which has misled many an uninformed person into believing that Mantrayāna is an 'erotic' form of Buddhism, (a conception as absurd as the assumption that Christian mysticism in the Middle Ages was an eroticized Christianity), has been prompted by the fact that "those who first set out on the path of Mantrayāna belong to a sensuous and sensual world and are, moreover, apt to seek enlightenment merely by making their passion for the charms of their female fellow-beings the path to it" [2]. Therefore, one hunts in vain for concrete "sex practices" in any one of the four Tantras, each of which in its own way contributes to the realization of the essential topics of Mantrayāna: the apprehension of no-thing-ness and the transfigurational technique. As Tsong-kha-pa declares: "The means utilized to make the sensuous and sensual the way is the apprehension of no-thing-ness and a transfigured existence. He who, in order to realize both these experiences, mostly depends on external acts of ritual, is a man of the Kriyātantra order. He who does not care too much for external acts and contemplation, both of which are equally distributed, is a man of the Caryātantra. He for whom contemplation gains in importance while ritual acts become less and less significant, is a man of the Yogatantra. He who without caring for ritual acts is capable of bringing about an unsurpassed integration, is a man of the Anuttarayogatantra" [3]. This gradation of the Tantras relates to their contents rather than to the individual who engages in them, because, as

---

[1] *SngSLNzh* 6ab.

[2] *Tskhp* III 38b.

[3] *Ibid.*

Tsong-kha-pa points out, "while there may be a greater or lesser interest in ritualistic acts and contemplative exercises, persons may also be interested in a path which is not suited to their capacities" [1].

The gradation of the experiential process towards an apex is not restricted to the Buddhist path as such nor to the division into four Tantras, for it is also the essential characteristic of the Anuttarayogatantra with its Two Stages, the Developing and the Fulfilment Stage.

The First or Developing Stage (*bskyed-rim, utpannakrama*) is preeminently a process of imagination. Imagination is the employment of past sensory and perceptual experiences, revived as images in a present experience at the ideational level. In fact, any past experience is potentially recallable, and therefore it is possible for feelings and emotions as well as cognitive processes to be imagined. The present experience, however, will not be in its entirety a reproduction of a previous one, but constitutes a new organization of material derived from past experience, sometimes in a pattern different from the original experience. Imagination is thus productive as well as re-productive, inasmuch as it suggests both memory and the image-making power. It also enriches and transforms the experience by its ability to make us conceive of that which is seen in fragments or on the surface as a complete and integral whole. Accordingly, to the purely sensuous content, there will be added intellectual elements that elevate imagination to the plane of inventive creation: artistic, musical, literary, and religious. It is natural that the greater the range of experience and the more fully developed the apperceptive background becomes by disengaging oneself from presuppositions and petty concerns, the wider and richer will be the imagination. The importance of imaginative thinking can never be overestimated, nor must it ever be underestimated, because it is the only means by which to counteract the trained incapacity of modern man, be he a specialist or a man in the street, preventing him from breaking old connections and for allowing new and vital linkages to emerge. However, imagination, if uncontrolled, becomes a vehicle for escape, but if properly directed it reveals values that are vital to human existence. Imagination is the very nature of the Developing Stage. This has been stated explicitly by Tsong-kha-pa [2]:

"As the Developing Stage is an imaginative process, it is a creation or a product of the mind not a physical phenomenon", and "Developing

[1] *Ibid.*, 39a.

[2] *Ibid.*, 369a.

Stage, Imagination Stage and Premeditated Integration Process are the names of the First Stage; Fulfilment Stage, Non-imagination Stage and Genuine and Spontaneous Integration Process those of the Second" [1]. These terms clearly show that the Developing Stage is essentially that of the generation of a new understanding and attitude. However, to let a new attitude and a new appreciation and understanding of a situation be born, the old one must die. In this process of self-development and integration the 'old' constitutes our self-imposed ficticity and limitation which we have accustomed ourselves to take for granted. To break these bounds is, certainly, a kind of death, and its dynamic aspect is referred to in the texts by such terms as 'immersing oneself in one's existentiality'. Here existentiality and immersion in it do not mean a mystical communion with transcendent being nor with an all-engulfing being in a sort of pantheism, but a process in which we open ourselves to a basic creativity which is our total being and which we have lost sight of because we have become involved in the objects of our appetance. The process of dying and of regeneration is described in terms of a cosmological myth, since an experience like the one in which old connections are broken is cataclysmic [2]. This poses the question of just what is the function of myth in the individual integrative process. The answer which L. A. Reid has given regarding the function of myth in religion applies here in full. He says that "if we do say that myths are attempts to say in imaginative language what is true, we have also to be careful not to assume that myths are cold, deliberate constructions, in imaginative form, representing the objective world. They are not scientific (or pre-scientific) cosmologies; they are not like early philosophical cosmologies, attempts to describe the origins and processes of nature on a large scale. Or at any rate they are not always this. Much more they seem to be dramatic and anthropomorphic projections expressing something of the deep and elemental tensions, conflicts and encounters taking place in our individual and collective lives. Perhaps much myth cannot be understood at all until it is related to the inner life of man. Much mythical cosmology is spontaneously (not instantaneously) projected dramatic construction, on a cosmic scale, of the drama of man's life on this earth and of the life-force of the spirit ceaselessly struggling to enclose and master the infinite" [3].

---

[1] *Ibid.*, 370a.

[2] *Ibid.;* VI 1, 7a seq. This myth is already found in the Aggaññasutta of the Pali Dīghanikāya.

[3] *Ways of Knowledge and Experience*, pp. 131 seq.

While the Developing Stage emphasizes the creative process and is the necessary preliminary experience (the apperceptive mass of Herbartian psychology), the Fulfilment Stage (*rdzogs-rim, sampannakrama*) signifies the emergence and recognition of the new situation with its appreciative understanding as a self-active and free-rising phenomenon. The Two Stages represent a definite mental activity on the part of existing systems of knowledge and the new understanding of the situation striving for recognition. The Two Stages in their interrelation show a certain similarity with Herbartian psychology, inasmuch as the cognitive or intellectual aspect is emphasized throughout. However, the intellectualism involved is different from that of Herbart as it is never divorced from an emotionally enriching quality because the structure of the noetic in Buddhism is such that it is never without its emotive component. The similarity with Herbart's conception of the working of the mind is evident from the explanation of the relation of the Two Stages, which Tsong-kha-pa gives [1]:

"If someone who wants to enjoy a banquet on the other side of a river cannot do so because he is prevented by the river, he may get into a boat and cross to the other side. Similarly, if someone wants to enjoy the riches of the Fulfilment Stage, but is unable to do so because he has been cut off by the river of his ordinary world of appearance and appetance for it, he may step into the boat of the Developing Stage and cross over to the other shore where the ordinary world of appearance and the appetance for it have left behind. Just as the crossing of the river by a boat is one process and the enjoyment of the banquet another, so also the Developing Stage is a process that prepares our mind for the birth of the Fulfilment Stage, but the enjoyment of the no-thing-ness and transfigured existence of the Fulfilment Stage is another process for which the experience of vibratory and creative processes is necessary. This shows that the Developing Stage must be pursued to its end and that alone it is not sufficient".

Inasmuch as the process described by the Two Stages serves to bring about a new orientation based on inner harmony, the purpose of the Developing Stage as the preliminary to this orientation is primarily the severance of all connections with the ordinary world of appearance and all appetance for it. This ordinary world of appearance relates to both the without and the within. Internally it is the self-complacency of utter

---

[1] *Tskhp* III 371a.

impersonality and is termed the 'common self-consciousness'. This self-consciousness is not aware nor concerned with man's humanity but with that which M. Heidegger has characterized as '*das man*' [1]. Here one is always master of a situation, one knows already everything and feels so reassured by finding oneself supported by widely prevailing opinion, but woe to him who dares to challenge this impersonality and insists on man's humanity. In order to overcome this complacency it is of primary importance to see oneself and the world in which one lives in a different light. This mode of seeing is both a 'seeing' and a 'feeling', but done in such a way that complacency has surrendered itself to a feeling of transfiguration. The literal translation of the term for this feeling (*lha'i nga-rgyal*) would be 'a God's pride', but literal translations rarely convey any meaning and because of the use of the word 'God' in our world there could be no greater misunderstanding than to see in this process some sort of deification. The latter elevates a concrete person into a superhuman being and expects wonders of him. Actually, therefore, it is an abuse of man, not an appreciation of humanity. There is an element of poetic justice in this process of deification that those who deify man are the first to be abused by the deified man. The feeling of transfiguration, on the other hand, is an emergence in freedom of mind and a more positive and revealing orientation towards the world in which one lives. The transition from the ordinary mode of seeing oneself and things to an appreciative one of transfiguration is a process of deepening insight."It has been said that the Developing Stage in which one imagines the world to be a divine mansion and the beings in it as transfigured beings ('gods', 'goddesses') counteracts the common way of appearance and the appetance for the latter; by familiarizing oneself with the appearance of the world as a divine mansion and of its inhabitants as transfigured beings, the ordinary mode of appearance is abolished; and by the certain feeling of being Akṣobhya or Vairocana or other deities, the common self-complacency is left behind. The transition from this self-complacency to the feeling of transfiguration is as follows: when one has reached real knowledge the former belief concerning one's identity is discarded and the idea that one is of a divine nature sets in. Similarly, when idea of being Akṣobhya or Vairocana or any other deity is established, the transition from common self-complacency to the feeling of transfiguration has been effected" [2]. Tsong-kha-pa then explains that

---

[1] *Sein und Zeit*. Halle, Max Niemeyer Verlag 1931, 3rd ed., p. 168.

[2] *Tskhp* III 375b.

the conquest of self-complacency is of primary importance and is the essential feature of the process, while the transfiguration of the world of appearance comes as the accompaniment of the conquest. That such a practice does not imply a negation of the world, but is a new orientation towards it and as such can never be a passing whim or affectation, is also clearly elaborated by Tsong-kha-pa [1]:

"The common way of appearance that is to be abandoned is not the world as it appears before our senses, but our feelings and ideas about it. The method of overcoming the common way of appearance and of the complacency we have towards it by the Developing Stage is neither the eradication of the potentiality of appearance as is done by the trans-worldly path, nor is it the weakening of this potentiality and the abolishing of the manifest form as is done by the worldly path. The conquest consists in the eradication of the common way of appearance and of the appetance for it by changing one's feelings and ideas about it when that which one has clearly imagined stands before one's mind in all its transparency. This happens when, in imagining the world and its inhabitants as a *maṇḍala* and in feeling oneself as transfigure, both the capacity for feeling transfigured and the *maṇḍala* are clearly present before one's mind. It is not enough to bring about a little change for a while, it must be a stable experience".

Although in the First Stage it is of utmost importance to learn to see the world as a divine mansion and the beings in it as gods and goddesses, and in so doing to be permeated by a feeling of transfiguration, it is equally important not to project these images of the imagination on concrete objects and persons. The purpose of all these practices is not to change the world nor to mould the persons according to an image, but to change one's attitude towards them and to find a new and more promising orientation. We must never forget that the knowledge which is valued in these practices, and which accompanies the process of re-orientation and integration, is never knowledge born of the desire to dominate and control others or the world in which we live. It is knowledge which expresses itself in the life of man and in an authentic manner, because it is born out of his nature which, though it cannot be grasped by essentialist categories, can be lived in the light of ultimate existential norms. For this reason the contemplation of no-thing-ness, the immediate apprehension of the fact that nothing exists in truth which by so existing

---

[1] *Ibid.*, 376a seq.

might warp and clog the free activity of the noetic in man, must be present at every step and turn. This has been insisted upon emphatically by Tsong-kha-pa [1]:

"The contemplation of no-thing-ness in the First Stage is a most important factor. The reason for this is that since the First Stage prepares the mind so that the full understanding which marks the Fulfilment Stage, can burst forth, without this contemplation of no-thing-ness this necessary readiness cannot be effected. This is so (I) because it has been stated that the contemplation of no-thing-ness is necessary from the very beginning inasmuch as many Tantras of the Mantrayāna declare that before one visualizes the circle of gods one has to speak the *mantra* which begins with the words *svabhāva* [2] and that the meaning of this *mantra* [3] is the contemplation and apprehension of the ultimate non-existence of an ontological status; (II) because in order to make the cognitive norm the path one's spiritual development it is necessary to contemplate no-thing-ness inasmuch as in the First Stage the three existential norms (of cognition, communication, and authentic being in the world) are made the path of spiritual growth; (III) because in order to familiarize oneself with the process of dying one must contemplate no-thing-ness inasmuch as on this Stage one has to understand the spiritual significance of birth, death and the intermediate stage; and lastly (IV) because in many Tantras and Sūtras it has been said more than once that everything, such as the visualization of the world as a divine mansion and of the beings in it as gods and goddesses, has to come out of a feeling of apparitionalness".

Once the Developing Stage has become a stable experience and the necessary preliminary experience is present, the Fulfilment Stage can be entered upon. This passes through five steps each of which is a purely psychological process even if it is described in terms of physical locations. After detachment from the preoccupation with the body has been established the first step (I) is one of an awareness of motility which is the cradle of cognizable mind. From this awareness develops an experience (II) which is likened to an emptying of the mind and which is in itself not determined at all. It is not just nothing, but an intensive mode of existing and acting, which underlies all actual cognition. When it achieves

---

[1] *Ibid.*, 398b.

[2] A long account on the significance of this *mantra* is found in *Tskhp* III 405b-408b.

[3] *Ibid.*, 443a.

determination its objective pole (III) is of the nature of an apparitional being, while its subjective pole (IV) is the cognition of its no-thing-ness. The last step (V) is the unity of apparitional existence and no-thing-ness. All this, however, is not an end in itself, it is a means to realize Buddhahood which is the most sublime idea man can have of man.

II.

THE TIBETAN SOURCES

CHAPTER SIX

THE GOLD-REFINERY BRINGING OUT THE VERY ESSENCE OF THE SŪTRA AND TANTRA PATHS

Praise to Guru Vajradhara!
My venerable Gurus [1], forbearing and without compare,
Who lead mankind as common men since in them they have gathered
The compassion of all Buddhas, rest
For ever as a crown upon my head.

May I be watched over by Vajradhara [2] sublime, Tilopa [3], Nāropa [4]
And the others, each the Guru of the next in spiritual succession,
With their peaceful and wrathful forms filling all the firmaments,
Yet never parting from the sphere of purest radiancy.

Mañjughoṣa [5], in whom are manifested both Guru and Buddhahood,
An ideal inspiring in which is condensed the spirituality
Of all the Buddhas in the infinite Buddha-realms,
Resides for ever in the lotus of my heart.

---

[1] Ye-shes rgyal-mtshan, the tutor of the Eight Dalai Lama (1758-1805 A.D.), had two Gurus to whom he was particularly indebted: Phur-long Ngag-dbang byams-pa and Grub-dbang bLo-bzang rnam-rgyal.

[2] Lit.: 'He who holds the Vajra'. He is a symbol for Buddhahood as it becomes accessible through making an inner experience of the teaching of the Buddha. The Vajra is a symbol of integration. Vajradhara is the spiritual progenitor of Tantrism.

[3] Tilopa, variously spelt Telopa, Tillipa, Tailopa (988-1069 A.D.) was the direct teacher of Nāropa.

[4] Nāropa, also known as Nāroṭapa, Nāḍapāda (1016-1100 A.D.) is famous for his assiduity and intellectual acumen. As the direct teacher of the Tibetan *lotsava* (translator) Mar-pa, who in turn was the teacher of Mi-la ras-pa (in *dge-lugs-pa* works often spelt as Mid-la ras-pa), he has been influential in the Tibetan development of Buddhism. On his life and work see my *The Life and Teaching of Nāropa*. Oxford, Clarendon Press, 1963.

[5] Mañjughoṣa is a symbol for Buddhahood as it expresses itself in the more intellectual form of an unbiased philosophical outlook. Conceived of in human

If you want to emulate the former saints in order to make this life worthwhile, as presenting a unique occasion [1], you must seek the path in which the Buddhas delight, without being attached to the riches of this world.

---

form he is the spititual forefather of those who developed the 'middle view' or the direct apprehension of the existentiality of all that is as being nothing in the sense that all that which we perceive cannot be reduced to an essence by virtue of which the things are what they are. It is an aethetic outlook rather than a theory about things. Although all the four major philosophical trends in Buddhism, the Vaibhāṣikas, Sautrāntikas, Vijñānavādins, and Mādhyamikas with their division into Svātantrikas and Prāsangikas, claim to adopt a 'middle view', the most strictly unbiased viewpoint is represented by the Prāsangikas who derive their tradition from Mañjughoṣa through Nāgārjuna and Āryadeva.

In paying homage to Vajradhara and Mañjughoṣa, Ye-shes rgyal-mtshan indicates which line of thought he is to elucidate: the philosophical outlook of the Prāsangikas and the enrichment by experience in Tantras.

[1] 'Unique occasion' is a comprehensive term which serves to indicate the absence of eight unfavourable conditions and to emphasize the importance of a life as a human being with its obligation to act in a human way. The eight unfavourable conditions which make the human way impossible are those of a denizen of hell, a spirit, an animal, a god, a savage, a man not in the full possession of his senses and faculties, a man with erroneous views, and a man disregarding the thoroughly humane doctrine of Buddhism. In *Ktsh* 73b seq. we are informed that "although, on the whole, these eight unfavourable conditions may not apply to us, they are nevertheless present in our minds and attitudes. That is to say, in spite of the fact that there are spiritual teachers and members of the Buddhist community, we are not different from savages, because we have no clear idea of what they stand for. Although we may be in the possession of the five senses, by not using them to practise true religion or by lacking in trust or in any other of the five faculties (*a*), we actually are not in the full possession of our senses and faculties. Although we may pretend to practise religion, apart from coming under the sway of the eight worldly concerns (*b*), we harbour erroneous views because we do not cultivate real religion after having become confident about the correctness of the Buddha's words. Although the Buddha's words are there, they become non-existent because we do not study and think about them. Because of the presence of great lust and passion we do not differ from spirits; because of the presence of intense anger and malice we do not differ from denizens of hell; and because of the presence of great dullness we do not differ from animals. To desire a state of concentration in which intelligence is not operative, is to make us equal to a long-living god. For these reasons we should be apprehensive and take care that we do not adopt a way characteristic of any one of the eight unfavourable conditions".

a) Trust, perseverance, inspection, concentration, and intelligence. Intelligence is always 'existential', it discriminates and appreciates and cognizes that which is important for man's life. It is a function and not a quality.

b) Gain and loss, fame and disgrace, praise and blame, pleasure and pain.

At this time when you follow the precious teaching of the Perfectly Enlightened One – it is a rare chance to hear his name even in countless aeons – you should not defeat your good fortune. [1]

Since there is no assurance that this life, which presents such a unique occasion once it has been won, will not end at any moment, you should dismiss all hopes and fears about a future and pledge yourself to realize true religion by focusing all your attention on it.

At this moment when you can still choose between (I) an ascent to either the higher forms of life [2] or to freedom, and (II) a descent into the depths of evil ways and forms of life [3], you should not remain in the dark about the chance you have.

Since in this evil age the life of man does not last long and since it is impossible to reach the limits of all that can be known, you should strive to attend to that which is essential instead of dabbling in too many things.

If you want to follow the path in which the Buddhas delight, you must accept the Buddha's words; emulate the true Buddha-sons [4] and follow the straight path of the Buddha's precepts.

In so far as in this evil age sentient beings, engulfed in utter darkness, often take to wrong ways, they first must find certainty about the unerring way by examining critically and with subtle logic the meaning of the Buddha's words [5].

On earth there was no greater sage than our incomparable teacher, Sākyamuni; and since there also was none greater in compassion you should study the Buddha's words.

Seeking unerring and firm certainty about the essential meaning of the Buddha's message, namely, the gradation of the path according to the three types of individuals, you must feel that upon which you concentrate.

---

[1] According to *Ktsh* 8a, true religious feeling "does not refer to merely muttering one's prayers or practising some charlantry as do soothsayers and Bon priests, but to counteracting passion-lust, anger-hatred, and bewilderment within us".

[2] The higher forms of life are those of a human being, a god, and a demon. Yet still higher is the realization of a deliverance from all forms of life and 'omniscience' which is the knowledge of the existentiality of all that is, the immediate apprehension and aesthetic appreciation of no-thing-ness.

[3] The lower forms of life are those of a denizen of hell, a spirit, and an animal.

[4] 'Buddha-sons' are those beings who strive for enlightenment in order to assist others in finding their way. Another designation for them is the Indian term Bodhisattva.

[5] Buddhism eschews any form of credulity. This it equates with stupidity. Although a Buddhist will have to accept the Buddha's words, he must do so critically.

The 'three types of individuals' does not refer to the unrelated practices of three different persons but to the progressive stages in the experiences of a single individual.

Just as a human being after birth gradually grows up and in time reaches the stages of childhood, youth and old age, so also this term 'three types of individuals' relates to a single man's levels of lowness, mediocrity, and superiority.

Further, by serving in a proper way by thought and deed spiritual friends [1] who are the undisputed source of all improvements, and by accomplishing what they tell you to do, you will prepare the ground for all achievements.

When you imbibe the nectar of the instruction in true religion which is so profound and so profuse [2], streaming suitably from the lips of true spiritual friends, in devotion and steadfastness, your body and mind will feel invigorated.

Again and again thinking about how difficult it is to obtain this human life as presenting a unique occasion and being an auspicious juncture [3],

---

[1] A 'spiritual friend' is anyone who helps us to develop our positive side. To serve him by thought means to trust his capacity to help us and to be grateful about that which he is doing for us. To serve him by deeds is to give him presents, to perform even menial work for him, but the highest form is to accomplish that which his teaching aims at. All these points have been elaborated upon at length in the vast *Lam-rim* (Stages on the Path) literature.

[2] 'Profound' relates to the philosophical outlook, and 'profuse' to the Bodhisattva activities.

[3] 'Auspicious juncture' refers to the five events which affect us directly and to another five accurring through others and thereby affecting us. The former are to be a human being, to be born in the central country (i.e., to live among educated persons), to be in the full possession of all one's senses, not to commit or instigate others to perpetrate heinous crimes, and to have confidence in the disciplinary code of the Buddha. See my *Jewel Ornament of Liberation*. London, Rider & Company 1959, pp. 15 seqq. According to *Ktsh* 70b their immediate profit to us is that "being present in him who follows the path they are the condition for his realization of rea lreligion". The five events occurring through others are the coming of a Buddha, the teaching of the doctrine, the continuation of that which has been taught, the readiness to assist others, and the dispensation of that which is necessary to us in compassion and kindness. According to *Ktsh* 71a the coming of a Buddha is to find and to continue in enlightenment. Finding enlightenment has a double significance, mentally it means to tear the veils of emotional instability and intellectual fog and to understand reality as it is; physically it relates to the event of the Buddha becoming the Englihtened One under the Bodhi-tree. The teaching of the doctrine is both the actual teaching and the study of it by any follower of Buddhism. The continuation of that which has been taught means that the path of seeing is born in him who

and how uncertain the time of death is, you must constantly keep alive the firm intention of not being preoccupied with this life and of concerning yourself with the hereafter.

What can you do when you have been reborn in the three evil forms of life [1], no longer with the power to determine where to be born when you die? Therefore, as long as you still have the power to choose you should strive to find the means to close the gates to evil births.

If you cannot stand a little heat and cold now, what will you do when you are boiled in molten lead or frozen in a fierce blizzard [2]? You must find shelter from such evil forces.

There is no other refuge able to protect you than the Three Infallible Jewels [3]. Therefore, take refuge in them from the depth of your heart.

---

makes a direct experience of that which has been taught and in particular it refers to the vividness and freshness of the experience of seeing reality divested of all that we are accustomed to heap upon it. The readiness to assist others means that he who has won the experience of reality becomes aware of the fact that others, like himself, have the capacity to win this experience and because of this awareness he protects and respects others. The dispensation of all that is necessary means the presence of patrons. "Although these features are not directly present in us, their likeness is available. There is the Guru who is like the Buddha; he teaches us religion, through him we practise it and an understanding of it is born in us; when this understanding is born we can teach others; and so we all are and have patrons".

[1] These are to be a denizen of hell, a spirit, or an animal. By this action man himself shapes his destiny. There is in Buddhism no transcendental hocus-pocus breaking into our life from somewhere in a manner we cannot and are not supposed to understand. The Buddha's claim upon the lives of men is that as a human being he has realized the uniqueness of man, his humanity. As is stated in *Ktsh* 7b: "Once we have fallen into evil forms of life even the Buddha has no chance to extract us. Man's action and Buddha-action are of equal strength."

[2] This is an allusion to the experiences in the hot and cold hells, all of which are vividly described in the *Lam-rim* literature.

[3] The Buddha, the Dharma and the Sangha. Their infallibility is not decreed by some outer agency, but is attested by the fact that they provide everything that is necessary for man to go his way safely. *Ktsh* 99ab states: "One has to take refuge in the Buddha, because he has all virtues and no defects. One has to take refuge in the Dharma in its aspect of revelation because it has been proclaimed by the Buddha, and in its aspect of a comprehensive understanding because even the Buddha achieved his goal through it. One has to take refuge in the Sangha, because they are the persons who will realize Buddhahood. In thus taking refuge two conditions must be fulfilled. We ourselves must be very frightened by the misery of evil forms of life, and there must be present the conviction that the power to protect us against this misery lies with the Three Jewels. The Pan-chen bLo-bzang chos-rgyan has stated the necessity of these two conditions being fulfilled, in the words:

Whatever there is of happiness and sorrow in the world has all come from your actions. At all times and on all occasions you should watch closely the gates to action, shun evil and do good.

When, through the formidable poison of the potentialities of the three basic emotional disturbances (passion-lust, aversion-hatred, and unknowing bewilderment), you act unwholesomely in body, speech and thought, you must purify yourself by the four expiatory vows which correspond to the four states of being afraid of evil, terrified by it, ashamed for it, and of being resolved to avoid it henceforth [1].

When by so striving you see the hysteria of the world as the antics of a drunkard tumbling into an abyss, and when without being attached to this life, the thought of what will become of you in a future life has been firmly established in your mind day and night, then the mental level of an inferior human being has been reached.

To take refuge is a trust:
We speak of taking refuge
When we go to shelter in the knowledge that
The power to protect is with the Triple Gem.
If these conditions are not fulfilled, it is
Like fire with naught to burn.

And the whole process is said to be as ineffective as a fire in a picture." The fact that the Buddha stands for the realization of knowledge and the abolishment of ignorance, both intellectual and emotional, the Dharma for that which makes this realization possible, and the Sangha for those who develop spiritually towards the goal, is clearly expressed in *Zhdm* 77ab: "For us the unfailing shelter which liberates us from our fear of Saṃsāra and its evil forms of life, is the Jewel of the Buddha, the Exalted One, whose nature is that he has completely given up what is to be given up and has understood thoroughly what is to be understood so that he is perfect in the possession of infinite virtues and in the absence of any defects. This shelter also is the Jewel of the Dharma which is of the nature of Truth purifying by becoming free from that which has to be eliminated either by seeing Truth or by attending to Truth seen; and it is also the Jewel of the community of saintly persons (Sangha) in whom the path towards the end of all misery develops."

[1] The four expiatory vows are related to the four powers of (I) making an atonement, (II) practising good as an antidote to evil, (III) desisting from evil, and (IV) the power of reliance. Although the order of these powers is enumerated in this way in the canonical texts (see my *Jewel Ornament of Liberation*, p. 121), Tsong-kha-pa makes the significant statement that in the practice of religion the last mentioned power comes first, as it implies the taking refuge in the Guru, the Buddha, the Darma, and the Sangha and the development of an enlightened attitude so important for following the Mahāyāna way. See *Tskhp* II 1, 215a seqq. The same order is also insisted upon is *Ktsh* 47a and other works.

Through thinking again and again about the general plight of the world you must acquire a feeling of disgust with it, for if you do not feel disgusted with the world in general no interest in deliverance from it can grow.

Since beginningless time you have roamed about in this world with its three spheres [1], fettered by your actions and emotional states, locked in the iron cage of the belief-in-an-*ens* [2] and harrassed by the tribulations of the three types of unsatisfactoriness [3].

Even if once in a while, whilst otherwise carried away by the turbulent rivers of birth, old age, disease and death and sinking deep into evil forms of life, you should have acquired the status of a being in happy forms of life, you will fall again through the power of your actions and emotional states, like an arrow shot into the sky by a boy.

To have obtained a human life is not a boon. First, when in the womb, you live in a heap of excrement and in dreadful gloomy darkness, are fed by bad-smelling and foul substances and are tormented by unbearable agonies.

When you pass from the womb through the uterine canal you feel pangs hard to bear. Then when you have reached the outer world and are touched, you suffer tortures as if being flayed and carved into pieces with a dagger.

Therefore a child is always crying, and when gradually he grows up and his muscles develop, many diseases attack him and continually cause him suffering.

The Buddha has said that whatever appears as a little happiness is but a change of misery. Therefore there is no real bliss in a human life.

---

[1] Our world is supposed to consist of three spheres, the world of sensuality comprising the human world as well as the hells and the realms of gods, the world of pure forms and the world beyond forms, where 'beyond' does not imply localization.

[2] Belief-in-an-*ens* is of a double nature, psychologically it is the belief in an ego or self as an entity. This belief has two forms, a 'coarse' and a 'subtle' one. The former is the acceptance of a Pure Ego, the latter that of a Central Event. On this distinction in Western psychology see C.D. Broad, *The Mind and its Place in Nature*. Physically this belief-in-an-*ens* assumes the existence of the entities of reality as such. This belief, too, is of two kinds. Its 'coarse' form involves the idealistic-mentalistic premise, its 'subtle' one assumes things to exist in truth.

[3] The three types of unsatisfactoriness are: the misery of misery, the misery of change, and the misery of conditioned existence. The two latter types are not misery as such, but derive their designation from their relation to the misery of misery which alone is misery.

Also to have been born as a god is not a boon. Being fettered by their actions and emotional states and urged on by their desires and lusts they find no rest. The stronger overpower the weaker; the armies of the demons trouble them and, in particular, when the five signs of death [1] are felt, they foresee themselves being born in lower forms and feel unbearable distress, sorrow and fright, like a fish thrown on dry land.

The Buddha has declared that the suffering of the gods afflicted by the signs of death is worse than the agonies in hell.

Even if you have become a god of the world of pure forms or of the realms beyond form you remain firmly fettered by your actions and emotional states, and even if you stay in concentration for a long time as if in deep dreamless sleep, when the impetus for this concentration has run out, you go down into the lower forms of denizens of hell, unhappy spirits, beasts, demons and into servitude, roaming about in these spheres.

When you have become a demon your mind is tormented by unbearable jealousy about the prosperity and splendour of the gods; you experience the misery of fights, quarrels, killings and mutilations, and there is no chance to see truth because of the thick veil of your actions.

Among the denizens of hell, spirits, and beasts there is never any bliss. There one is always tormented by hundreds of pains, by thirst, hunger, heat, and cold. There also one must carry burdens and endure many other hardships. When even to hear about this misery frightens you, what will you say when you actually see and experience it?

In brief, in all stations of Saṃsāra the deceiver 'belief-in-an-*ens*' has made his home in the hearts of all beings. Deluded by the mistaken idea of misery being bliss and by the fallacy of what does not exist in truth appearing to do so, you are imprisoned in an endless cycle of births.

Fettered tightly by the craving for and clinging to objects, like a moth attracted by the light of a lamp, you roam about taking delight in places of misery that are your undoing.

Having entered this prison of the triple world [2], extending from the top of the universe to the hells at the bottom, and being heavily fettered by your actions and emotional states, you are continuously racked with the pain of potential misery.

---

[1] They are: the god's dress becomes soiled, his garlands of flowers fade, perspiration breaks forth from his arm-pits, a foul smell rises from his body, and he is dissatisfied with his throne. See *Tskhp* XIII 138b; XIV 1, 75b; *Zhdm* 143a seqq.

[2] See note 1, p 83.

Therefore the Victorious One has declared that all situations, all forms of existence, and all enjoyable riches of the world exemplify the Truth of Misery.

When you think thus about the status of the world and when, day and night, through dread, fear, disgust and a feeling of repulsion the intention to find deliverance has been firmly established in your mind, the level of a mediocre being has been reached.

Then, when again and again you think that, since beginningless time, sentient beings as infinite as the sky have been your mother [1] and are indeed your old mother to be treated with kindness, you must develop the noble intention that you surely will have to deliver all beings, like your old mother, from Saṃsāra through loving-kindness and compassion.

Since only the teaching of true religion can deliver beings, you must develop firmly a precious enlightened attitude which means that you must reach the citadel of Buddhahood in order to impart such religion to sentient beings.

When there is present this wondrous fortitude of a noble intention which has been brought into being by loving-kindness, compassion and

---

[1] To think of sentient beings as being our mother is of particular importance and is one of the 'Sevenfold Cause-Effect Relation' topics that have first been formulated by Dīpankara Śrījñāna (Atīśa). As Tsong-kha-pa in *Tskhp* XIII 182b seq., and XIV 1, 88b seqq., points out "Perfect Buddhahood derives from an attitude directed towards enlightenment, the latter from a noble intention, the latter from compassion, the latter from loving-kindness, the latter from repaying one's indebtedness, the latter from gratefulness, and the last from seeing all beings as one's mother". He then declares that, while loving-kindness and compassion do not necessarliy stand in a cause-effect relation, the consideration of sentient beings as one's mother and all that which leads up to loving-kindness is causal to the noble intention of feeling for others and developing an enlightened attitude. Above all, "since the ultimate counteragent (of the aversion and indifference to sentient beings) is the feeling of motherliness, to think of all beings as mothers, remembering, being aware of and repaying their kindness, effect friendliness and esteem, and the result is a loving-kindness which holds sentient beings dear as a mother does her only child. And this leads to compassion" (XIV, 1, 90b). Tsong-kha-pa stresses the active aspect of Buddhism when he continues: "When it is quite sufficient that one develops the desire to attain Buddhahood for the sake of sentient beings when compassion is felt after one has trained one's mind gradually in the above manner, why should one demand a noble intention in between? The answer is that, while the Śrāvakas do have an unlimited feeling of kindness and compassion directed towards the desire that all sentient beings meet with happiness and be freed from misery, the *obligation* to make all sentient beings attain happiness and become free from misery is found only with a Mahāyānist. Hence the necessity to develop a noble intention in fortitude" (*ibid.*, fol. 90b seq.).

an enlightened attitude, and when it never weakens in its endeavour to deliver sentient beings from the ocean of Saṃsāra so that you continue to act as a son of Buddha with far-reaching effects, then the level of a superior man has been reached.

When you set out on the Mahāyāna path, you have been prompted by a precious enlightened attitude [1] which never weakens in its care for others through the fortitude of the noble intention to consider them more important than yourself; moreover you do not fall a prey to selfishness by not being attached to this life. And so by thinking of what will become of you later, and by not being involved in this world but concerned with deliverance from such involvements it becomes important for you to know the division into outlook, meditative practice, and conduct as well as into the starting point, path, and goal.

In regard to the division into outlook, meditative practice, and conduct, there are many varieties due to the gradation of beings according to their temperaments, likings, tendencies and intellectual capacities, as well as to that of the spiritual courses.

First of all, the Buddhas and wise Buddha-sons have extolled (I) the view which sees clearly all concrete things as impermanent, unstable and perishing each moment; (II) the view which is absolutely certain that all affect-arousing processes are merely misery because they are controlled by actions and emotional states, while there is no Self ruling the psycho-somatic constituents, – for this problem has been investigated by clear and subtle reasoning; and (III) the 'correct worldly outlook' which is the certainty that all concrete things in general, and whatever there is of happiness and sorrow in particular have come about through inherent causes and conditions. Since there is no effect without a cause the relation between cause and effect regarding our actions is infallible [2].

When you have found this certainty of so seeing things, you must with an unswerving mind focus all your attention on this existential mode of

[1] 'Precious enlightened attitude' indicates the Mahāyānist readiness to be of help to others. This readiness to help manifests itself in the effort to become a living example for others, but not in meddling with the affairs of others in an ill-advised philanthropic sentimentality. The term 'enlightened attitude' has been interpreted variously. Asanga seems to have emphasized the content, while Nāgārjuna and others stressed attitudinal readiness. Both interpretations, though favouring the latter, have been given in *Ktsh* 171b seq. 'Precious' specifies the Mahāyānist readiness.

[2] That is to say, our bad actions bring misery upon us, while our positive actions will help us forward.

impermanence, unsatisfactoriness and non-entitativeness. Having found such certainty through trustworthy revelation and clear reasoning you must concentrate properly on the nature of the thirty-seven elements leading to enlightenment, what they refer to, what their observable qualities are, how to work with them, and what their outcome is. They are the four topics for inspection [1], the four attempts at rejection and acquisition [2], the four types of deep concentration [3], the five controlling powers and the five forces [4] such as confidence and the rest, the seven members of enlightenment [5], and the eight sectors of the Noble Path [6].

When you thus practise outlook and meditation you must watch the three gates to action [7] in all your ways of movement and rest by means of inspective techniques and remain indefatigable in avoiding evil and doing good.

Our incomparable Teacher (the Buddha) has guarded like the apple of his eye the limits within which pitiful beings move. Hence, when the proper observance of the limits set by the Prātimokṣa [8], the foundation

---

[1] 'Inspection' stands here for keeping the perceptual situation as constant as possible and inspecting the objective constituent of this situation as equitably as possible. The four objective constituents of such a perceptual situation are: that which constitutes our physical existence, feeling, dispositions and that which we call the whole of reality taken entitatively.

[2] They are: to give up the evil and unwholesome that has already arisen and not to allow more to rise, to create and then to increase the good and wholesome in opposition.

[3] These are those which are prompted by strong interest, perseverance, disposition and investigation.

[4] Confidence, perseverance, inspection, meditative discoursing and intelligence. The latter is always discriminative. It is an appreciative function bearing on man's existence with the active, temporal contingency that comes with it. The distinction between five controlling powers and five (stable) forces respectively emphasizes the nature of meditation as a modifiable process. The 'controlling powers' direct the course of contemplation and inform it, while the 'forces' make it continue by permeating it.

[5] Inspection, intelligence, energy, enthusiasm, relaxation, meditative concentration and equanimity.

[6] Right view, conception, speech, action, life, exertion, inspection and concentration.

[7] Body, speech and thought.

[8] The Prātimokṣa is part of the Buddhist Disciplinary Code and deals with the different status and obligations of the religious-minded. Mainly seven groups are counted (the eighth or those who keep a temporary vow of fasting for a day or so, being insignificant for practising religion): monks and nuns, female religious

of the teaching, is made the starting point, the experience of that which you practise will become deeper and deeper; but when you disregard this foundation, whatever you try will fail. To hope that the experience will deepen and the practice proceed is like expecting branches to grow where no tree has been planted and to build a house without there being a foundation.

When you have laid a firm foundation for the path, you attempt to achieve the conduct of the Buddha-sons, which has far-reaching effects, the practice of outlook, meditation, and conduct being as follows:

As to outlook you have to follow the 'middle path' which is unhampered by the extremist opinions of eternalism and nihilism [1].

As to meditation you have to practise tranquillity and insight undisturbed by avidity and listlessness [2].

As to conduct you have to learn about and practise the six perfections [3].

In order to gain this outlook which avoids the extremes of eternalism and nihilism you must with the help of instruction by those who are in the spiritual tradition, critically and subtly examine the meaning of those Sūtras which reveal the direct meaning propounded by the Buddha, after you have divided the scriptures into those revealing the direct meaning

---

students, novices, both male and female, and lay people, also male and female. In the Tibet of today (even before the Communist annexation) the tradition of the status of nuns and female religious students has long since been extinct. The so-called nuns are not full nuns, but female novices respecte dfor their way of life.

[1] It is important to note this definition, because in gaining an unbiased outlook and viewpoint from which it is possible to see things as they are, apart from our appetites and conjectures, the gradation of the path or the intellectual training of Buddhism becomes most conspicuous. To put it somewhat simply, Buddhism passes from something like realism through idealism-mentalism to a beyond-idealism.

[2] Tsong-kha-pa in *Tskhp* XIV 1, 147b seqq., quotes the definition of avidity in the *Abhidharmasamuccaya*, stating that it participates in the nature of the basic emotional tendency of passion-lust by following up that which is pleasant and agreeable and preventing the mind from coming to rest. For this reason it is an obstacle to tranquillity.

Listlessness must be distinguished from that gloominess and despondency which participate in the basic intellectual emotion of bewilderment or the going astray of the mind, although listlessness springs from this state easily. While gloominess is thoroughly negative, listlessness may well occur in positive attitudes.

[3] Liberality, ethics and manners, patience, strenuousness, meditative concentration and intelligence. On this latter term see also above note 4, p. 87.

and those suggesting it [1]. You must find an unerring and firm certainty, otherwise you will, as a rule, become confused and fall into the abyss of wrong views.

Since that which has fettered the sentient beings of the three spheres in Saṃsāra since beginningless time, is the straying into the 'belief-in-an-*ens*', you must recognize the real evil of this wandering which constitutes that belief. Having completely destroyed the mode of believing inherent in this erratic belief-in-an-*ens*, you must become certain that the existentiality of things [2] is not an entitative existence in truth. Whatever appears before the six senses does so because of its inherent causes and conditions. When you judge this appearance of infallible relatedness as being something nonexistent you fall into the nihilistic extreme; and when through the un-knowing fallacy of the belief-in-an-*ens* you take things as they appear to exist as such, you fall into the eternalistic extreme. Whatever you try will fail when you fall into the abyss of either nihilism or eternalism.

For instance, when you want to catch a poisonous snake you will succeed if you seize it by the tail and fling its vicious poisonous head backwards. But you endanger yourself if you grasp it by the head. Therefore, when you try to win an unbiased outlook you harm yourself if you fall into the nihilistic or eternalistic extremes.

When you seek the middle path avoiding the extremes of eternalism and nihilism, the very moment you have found it the world crumbles and you are quickly delivered from the ocean of existence.

---

[1] For the Mādhyamikas those texts which deny the existence of things in truth state the direct meaning of the Buddha's message, while those which deal with various strata of the mind are merely suggestive. For the Vijñānavādins it is the other way round. Ye-shes rgyal-mtshan, of course, adopts the Mādhyamika view.

[2] The 'existentiality of things' is the fact that they do not exist in truth as absolute entities. Existentiality (*gnas-lugs*) is synonymous with the Sanskrit word *śūnyatā*, which I translate by no-thing-ness in order to bring out its character of absolute negation (*med-dgag*). For those of us who are geared to thinking in terms of things the idea that there should be no things and that we yet deal with them in everyday life is difficult to grasp. This raises the problem as to whether thinking in terms of things is not a peculiar kind of (cultural) conditioning that cannot claim validity for all. The distinction between a 'co-emergent belief in things' and a 'postulationally defined belief in things' which is concisely stated in *Ktsh* 198a, bears a close resemblance to what C.D. Broad, *The Mind and its Place in Nature*, p. 215 discusses under the heading 'The quasi-Belief about the Sensum' and on pp. 216 seq. under 'The Categorical Factor in Sense-Perception'.

The two facts, firstly that all things from the beginning have been void of any eternal principle through which they become what they are, and secondly that the relation between cause and effect is infallible, are not contradictory but mutually compatible. Therefore all that which appears is nothing and that which is nothing appears. To find this middle path or the unity of appearance and no-thing-ness is to gain the outlook praised by the Buddha.

When you have thus abolished all imputations [1] through an unbiased outlook you must focus your attention indefatigably on the primal existentiality of all that is.

Since when meditating on the existentiality of mind-in-itself, avidity and listlessness, like enemies, create obstacles, you must keep firmly to inspection and reflection [2].

If you do not stop thinking in terms of subject and object and of a naive attitude towards objects believed to exist in truth, you will not be able to see the existentiality of mind-in-itself. This may be illustrated as follows: If at night when you look at a wall-painting the flame of the lamp is violently shaken by the wind, you do not see the picture clearly, but if the flame is not stirred and shines steadily you see the figures in the picture clearly. The existentiality of mind-in-itself is clearly seen from a non-dichotomic, brilliantly clear and well-focused point of concentration. Therefore, during meditation there must be neither avidity nor listlessness.

When you have overcome properly the slightest tendency [3] to these two states by practising a state of clearness, which is brilliant, non-dichotomic and well-focused, you ascend gradually through the nine

---

[1] 'Imputations' are best described as a set of propositions which between them 'define' a certain general concept, for instance, the notion of a Self or a Physical Object. See *Tskhp* XIV, 1, 167a seq.

[2] Avidity and listlessness make proper concentration impossible. The former prevents the proper focusing of the mind on the object of contemplation, and the latter upon its clarity. In order to counteract these inimical forces two processes are necessary. These are 'inspection' and 'reflection'. As is stated by Tsong-kha-pa in *Tskhp* XIV, 1, 143b seq.: "Concentration means to have the mind well focused. For this purpose two processes are necessary, the one not allowing the mind to swerve from its object (i.e., to keep the perceptual situation as constant as possible), the other knowing whether or not the mind swerves from its object. The former is inspection, the latter reflection". Similarly also in *Tskhp* XIII 303b, and *Ktsh* 180b.

[3] According to *Ktsh* 180b a slight indication of listlessness is felt when the intensity or interest in concentrating on the object of contemplation weakens.

stages of mind [1]. As soon as you begin to think effortlessly, you pass into a state of composure without strain or stress, like an eagle rising in the sky. Then, by gradually establishing the continuity of this status, your whole body becomes permeated by supple vibrations and body and mind become at ease and feel pleasant and happy. At this moment the tranquillity-meditation stage has been reached. On whatever positive object you may concentrate, it will stay unshakably, and when you let go of it, it will pass away like a wisp of cotton blown by the wind. Body and mind are continually supple and blissful. Such qualities as supersensible cognitions, deep concentrations and all types of understanding available on the higher paths and levels derive from this tranquillity-meditation stage.

---

[1] The nine stages of the mind describe the process of concentrating. They are, as explained by Tsong-kha-pa in *Tskhp* XIV 1, 153b seq., (I) to withdraw mind from the outer objects and direct it towards an inner object, an idea or image; (II) not to allow mind to stray away but to keep it with the inner object; (III) when mind is about to let the object slip from its inspection and turn to the outer objects, to become aware of it and tie the mind to the object of inspection; (IV) to deepen the inspective awareness; (V) to take delight in concentration by having thought about its virtues; (VI) to calm any unhappiness about concentration by considering distraction as a defect; (VII) to calm any tendency towards cupidity, unhappiness, gloominess, sleepiness and so on; (VIII) to make efforts to let mind pass into a state of effortlessness; and (IX) to continue in equanimity when one has entered a state of composure.

The nine stages are related to six powers and four procedures. The six powers are (a) studying (lt.: hearing the instructions from a teacher); (b) thinking about what one has heard; (c) inspecting the object of one's thought situation; (d) reflecting on what one inspects; (e) persevering in this activity; and (f) becoming familiar with the subject-matter.

The four procedures are (1) to force oneself to fix one's mind on the object of contemplation; (2) occasionally to stop the fixing of the mind on its object; (3) as the case may be to have mind fixed on its object without interruption; and (4) to have mind automatically fixed on its object. The nine stages, six powers and four procedures are related to each other in the following way:

I	a	1 (a, b)
II	b	
III, IV	c	2 (c, d)
V, VI	d	
VII, VIII	e	3
IX	f	4

When you have thus won an imperturbable tranquillity you must examine again and again with discriminative and appreciative acumen the existentiality of mind-in-itself and strengthen your certainty about it[1].

Then when, through the power of this discriminative acumen, physical and mental peace have been won, and when you have reached the most superb concentration that remains well-focused, you acquire the understanding and comprehension of the insight-meditation stage which sees the existentiality of mind-in-itself most clearly. This has been greatly praised by the Buddha as the meditation in which tranquillity and insight unite.

After that, by practising this meditation continuously, you reach the higher paths and levels with their non-dichotomic awareness which begins with the 'path of seeing' [2].

While thus applying yourself to the practice of outlook and meditation you must lead a life which expresses itself in the fulfilment of the six perfections, the unique way travelled by all Buddha-sons. Each perfection is subdivided into six, and whilst diving into the ocean of the conduct of the Buddha-sons you must adopt a way of living which is salutary in every respect.

Thus the experience of being prompted by an enlightened attitude and of delving into the conduct of the Buddha-sons, indicates the common road of all Buddha-sons whether they follow the auspicious path of the Sūtras or that of the Tantras.

When you set out on the Vajrayāna path after having made the above mentioned road of the Buddha-sons your starting point [3], the practice of outlook, meditation, and conduct is as follows:

---

[1] This distinguishes Tibetan (and its source: Indian) Buddhism from the peculiar Chinese form, the Hva shang meditation, as it is called in the Tibetan texts, where contemplation is said to consist in staring into empty space with a blank mind.

[2] Although it may be claimed that Buddhism teaches one path, this path is subdivided into five stages, each being termed a path. These are: the path of preparation, the path of linking (that which one has learned with the supreme stage) the path of seeing, the path of attending to that which has been seen, and the path of no more learning. The last three 'paths' are the higher ones. These higher paths proceed through ten spiritual levels.

[3] The *Lam-rim* literature is unanimous in asserting that the Vajrayāna path has to be travelled, and it also insists that the practice of the 'common' path has to precede the study of Vajrayāna. See for instance *Zhdm* 205b, *Tskhp* III 40a, 119b seqq. The idea that the Tantras can be understood without first having studied and comprehended the 'Sūtra literature' properly – a claim put forward

A mode of seeing which is free from straying into the subject-object dichotomy with its belief in external objects as existing in truth, is outlook [1];

The unity of profoundness and clarity is meditation; and

Conduct is called the 'triple dalliance'; that is, to conceive of your dwelling place, your food and clothes and whatever else you enjoy as a god's sacred vessel, clothes and enjoyments, none of them arousing emotionally tinged unbalancing responses.

This transfiguration of all that appears into vast purities is the practice of outlook, meditation, and conduct as detailed in the Kriyā-, Caryā-, and Yogatantras [2].

When mind and body feel invigorated and when you set out on the Anuttarayoga path [3], the practice of outlook, meditation, and conduct is as follows:

You have to find certainty as to the Mahāmudrā [4]. This is the view in which the reality of all entities, initially free from the subject-object mode of thinking, and the naive belief about things as existing in truth, indivisibly unite with their cognition in great bliss.

Meditation has to be done by focusing your attention on the pure radiant light. In contemplating the deities of the vast *maṇḍalas*, in which

---

by many scholars – is as preposterous as the assumption that one can be an expert nuclear physicist without having studied physics and mathematics.

[1] Although this statement looks like the idealist's claim which denies that there are external physical objects to cause our sensations, there is a marked difference between Buddhist and Western idealism. While Western idealists insist on the conclusion that all reality is mental, the Buddhists do not subscribe to this theory. It may be true that my experience of the world is a mental phenomenon, but this does not entail that the world itself is mental. *GC* III 76b seq. clearly rejects the thesis that chairs and tables are 'mental' only. Here, however, the statement means that one grasps the fact clearly that neither a subject nor an object exist in truth.

[2] These three Tantras are known as the 'Lower Tantras'. In a certain way they are preparatory of the Anuttarayogatantra, the 'Highest Form of an Integration Process'. In Buddhism *yoga* does not mean a union with the Absolute. It is true, *yoga* means 'union' also in Buddhism, but this 'union' is relational and cognitive, not substantial.

[3] See the preceding note.

[4] This is one of the few Eastern terms which I have left untranslated (and incidentally given in the Sanskrit form, because the Tibetan term *phyag-rgya chen-po* or *phyag-rgya chen-mo* might present some pronunciation difficulties). It is a term for 'noetic union' where the noetic act is grounded in the knowing agent and stretches forth as an empty relational form to be terminated by the object having its own ground. There is thus existential diversity with formal unity.

they (and you) reside, you have to feel the pride of being divine like them[1]. In this way both the coarser and subtler forms of the unifying process have to be practised.

Conduct must be endowed with four purities; the transfiguration of your dwelling place (into the Buddha realm); of your being (into that of a deity); of your possessions (into sacred vessels of worship); and of your actions (into modes of taking into consideration the actual needs of the moment).

Thinking that whatever appears is a divine realm, you have to live in such a way that whatever you do expresses the knowledge of the fitness of action.

The above mentioned triple way constitutes the practice of outlook, meditation, and conduct as done by a man occupied with the First Stage [2].

---

[1] In more precise terms this means that through meditation we overcome our dull complacency in which we take such a pride in ordinary life ('blunt facts and no fiddle-sticks') and become sensitively alive and aesthetically moved. The 'divine pride' (*lha'i nga-rgyal*) is not just a higher form of 'common conceitedness' (*tha-mal-pa'i nga-rgyal*). Rather it indicates the feeling of transfiguration and points to the dignity of man. If man wants to go his way to his humanity, he must be convinced of his dignity as man; to conceive of himself as somebody's chattel will never assist him in finding his way. Tsong-kha-pa is quite explicit on this point. See *Tskhp* III 46b; 376b.

[2] The First Stage (*bskyed-rim*) which relates to the technique of conceiving oneself as a god (*lha*) is a thoroughly imaginative-transfigurative process, by no means is it to be considered as a deification of man which serves as a means of despising all others. This is quite clear from the remarks by Tsong-kha-pa, *Tskhp* III 369ab. The purpose is to counteract 'common appearance' and 'appetance'. The former relates to the naive assumption we have about appearance, to believe that whatever makes itself known to us by appearing exists so in truth and is not defined by a set of propositions. The latter denotes our feelings and moods about that which appears. As a rule, appearance and appetance never work separately, and it needs hard training to separate the two. The mixed state of appearance and appetance is 'the worldly way', as the Buddhist texts call this situation. In this case there is little of that which we would call a point of view from where to apprehend things as they really are, because we are too much concerned with our practical presuppositions: things are there to be manipulated and human beings also are there for a purpose. Once we attempt to detach ourselves from our practical concerns and situations and begin to free ourselves from our assumptions and involvements we set out on a 'transworldly way', as the Buddhist texts call this phenomenon. Following this path we enter a realm that is richer in content and broader in horizon. The religious language born out of its immediate experience calls it a divine realm in which divine persons move. In the abstract language of psychology and philosophy this means that a man comes nearer his possibilities

When your ability to discriminate and appreciate has been perfected, you must, through an awareness which itself is great bliss, see the existentiality of all that is. This is the no-thing-ness in which all tendencies towards believing in the true existence of all sense objects have disappeared.

Immersing yourself in your existentiality you must attune yourself to the existential norms (regulating your thoughts, communication with others, and living in the world) of the Dharma-, Sambhoga-, and Nirmāṇakāyas [1], when (I) you meditate on the semblance- and reality-radiances together with the experiences like waking up, going to sleep, and dying, and when (II) you ordinarily go to sleep, dream, and wake up again.

When your conduct is regulated by the three modes: (I) belief in that which is as existing in truth, (II) belief in that which is as not existing in truth, and (III) belief in that which is as utterly non-existing in truth, then the fact that you have reached the citadel of unity and integration indicates your status of the highest being, comparable to a precious jewel.

Having become the greatest on the great path and the foremost of the Buddha-sons, the spiritually advanced persons who occupy themselves with the Second Stage [2] practise keenly and energetically the conduct mentioned above because it guarantees enlightenment in one short lifetime during this evil age.

In the division into a starting point, path, and goal, there are also many varieties according to the intellectual acumen and the intentions

---

from which he usually tries to escape in order to become submerged in an anonymous and amorphous mass. Under no circumstances is this First Stage to be considered as a kind of concretization. This is clearly evident from Tsong-kha-pa's statement in *Tskhp* III 375b seq.

[1] Dharmakāya, Sambhogakāya, and Nirmāṇakāya are technical terms describing structures that are relational rather than substantial. A distinction must be made between their ultimate relational forms and their apprehendable aspects belonging to the 'path' or developmental process. They are existential norms which we must try to live up to by following the path. Dharmakāya is a cognitive relation, Sambhogakāya a communicative one, and Nirmāṇakāya is best described as a coming-into-the-world authentically.

[2] The Second or Fulfilment Stage (*rdzogs-rim*) is the 'felt' knowledge in the First Stage. Its 'Fulfilment', which comes about through five phases, does not involve a concretization of that which has been developed. The god that has been developed is not idolized but, instead, is cognized as that for which he or she stands. See *Tskhp* III 370b.

of individuals as well as to the gradation of the spiritual courses. Briefly they can be subsumed under (I) a general and (II) a specific division.

(I) In the general division the starting point is the unity of the two truths [1]; the path the unity of fitness of action and intelligence [2]; and the goal the unity of a dual pattern [3].

The two truths relate to ultimate and conventional truths. The Buddha has declared that the ultimate truth is that all entities of reality since beginningless time have been void of any principle existing in truth through which they are what they are. He also insisted that whatever appears as an object to the senses of the sentient beings of the three spheres is a straying into the fallacious belief about things as really existing. This belief constitutes the conventional truth.

The appearance of things in the accustomed way and their existentiality as being nothing because void of any truth-principle, are not two separate facts but one. If the two truths were separate, these entities of reality could never have been in a state of judgment suspension from their very beginning and whatever one would see would be make-belief. Thus the Buddha has said. And regarding this existentiality the *Prajñāpāramitā* texts have loudly voiced the statement:

> Non-dual, inseparable into two.

The auspicious path on which fitness of action and intelligence unite, is the only path to be travelled by the Buddha-sons. If ever fitness of action and intelligence part you are unable to advance to the Buddha-level, just as a bird with only one wing cannot fly up in the sky.

---

[1] Ultimate and conventional. The former relates to seeing things as they really are, divested from our assumptions and appetites; the latter is the commonsense view.

[2] Linguistic translations render the two technical terms, *thabs* and *shes-rab* (*upāya* and *prajñā*), by 'Means' and 'Wisdom'. These linguistic translation which follow a mechanical dictionary method completely and deliberately ignore that which the texts themselves have to say. *Shes-rab* (*prajñā*), like our 'intelligence', is analytical and when disciplined becomes capable of pursuing Truth and ascending the highest summits from where things may be seen as they really are. In this sense, it is more than mere intelligence. It is discriminative, appreciative, and always bears on man's existence as a whole. Above all it is a dynamic function, not a static quality. However, alone it is useless. It needs a moral frame. This is referred to by 'fitness of action'. It is not mere naive expediency, that is, to do what seems obvious, easy or convenient. It means to be aware of the actual situation and to use intelligence concerning that which needs to be done here and now.

[3] Cognitive readiness and communicative relations.

The method utilized to unite fitness of action and intelligence is to practise the six perfections when you imitate the Buddha-sons. That is to say, prompted by an enlightened attitude you must practise liberality, observe ethics and manners, show patience, be assiduous, pass into a state of composure and then use your sense of critical appraisal. Whatever you do in the above practice must be inspired by an enlightened attitude and supported by a cognition which sees all that appears as but an apparition, and so is indirectly aware of its non-existence in truth. If there is no such support by an enlightened attitude there is no chance to set out on the Mahāyāna path, at best you will follow the Hīnayāna way. And so the lord of saints has taught that if we do not return the kindness which all sentient beings in the six modes of life have shown to us by having been our father and mother, we deviate into the Hīnayāna way. Therefore, when you strive to develop an enlightened attitude you must do so with great loving-kindness.

Since you are fettered by the ties of determinate characteristics [1] if you do not look at things from a viewpoint which understands the existentiality of all that is as not existing in truth, you are powerless to move and to set out on the path to freedom, like a bird to whose leg a stone has been tied.

Inasmuch as through fitness of action the functional patterns, and through intelligence the existential-cognitive pattern, are realized, it is necessary to travel the path on which fitness of action and intelligence unite in order to find the unity of these patterns.

The goal or the unity of the two patterns is the unity of the reality [2] and manifestation patterns [3]. The former is said to be both ultimate [4] and cognitive [5]. Here, ultimate pattern means to have attained a status

---

[1] Determinate qualities, exactly as the senses and specific introspections indicate, are transitory; but being in 'the centre of consciousness' man is naturally attached to them. Every attachment is a fetter.

[2] Dharmakāya.

[3] Rūpakāya, consisting of the Sambhogakāya and the Nirmāṇakāya.

[4] Svābhāvikakāya.

[5] Jñānadharmakāya. In most cases, especially so in Sanskrit texts, the various literary documents speak of Dharmakāya only. Almost always its cognitive aspect as an indeterminate relational form is meant. Due to the fact that the texts use the word Dharmakāya for both Jñānadharmakāya and Svābhāvikakāya, many translations from Sanskrit texts give a wrong picture of what is actually meant by them. The Dharmakāya is real and existent, the Svābhāvikakāya is real but not existent. Everything existent is transitory, so is the Dharmakāya as Jñānadharmakāya.

that is of the nature of utter purity because emotional instability and intellectual fog have been abolished through the continued practice of outlook, meditation, and conduct by the Buddhas whilst on the path of learning [1]. The cognitive pattern, on the other hand, denotes the immediate awareness of everything knowable by virtue of having travelled the path for countless aeons. Both these patterns are referred to as the Dharmakāya.

The manifestation patterns are also twofold: communicative [2] and sensible [3].

The former is the permanent presence of an ideal endowed with all major and minor symbols, continually voicing the message of true religion which resounds as long as the sky exists so as to impart the intention of the Buddha continuously to the excellent Buddha-sons who control the ten spiritual levels. This ideal never leaves the pure Buddha realms which appear in their true nature (as not existing in truth as such), when through the power of the two piles of knowledge and merits, accumulated during countless aeons, the tendency towards straying into the belief in things as existing in truth has been abolished.

The latter, namely, the sensible manifestation pattern, is the effortless manifestation on behalf of the aspirants, according to temperaments, likings and interests of countless beings.

These two functional patterns (known as Sambhogakāya and Nirmāṇakāya respectively) are not separate entities nor do they come about in succession. Just as through the concentration called the Diamond-like

---

[1] The path of learning comprises the following stages which are called paths: the path of linking that which one has learned with the path of seeing, the path of seeing reality as it is, and the path of attending to and deepening the experience of that which one has seen. It continues up to the path of no more learning or Buddhahood realized. The objective reference of the cognition involved varies according to the three spiritual courses, that of the Śrāvakas, Pratyekabuddhas, and Bodhisattvas. For the Śrāvakas the objective reference is the non-existence of a Self even in its subtle form. The term 'subtle' is used in order to exclude the belief in a Self as a Central Event. Such a Self was recognized by the Vātsīputrīyas who, like all other Buddhists, rejected the 'coarse' belief in a Self or a Pure Ego Theory. The Pratyekabuddhas realize in addition to the non-existence of a Self the fact that external objects do not exist apart from their being experienced and that therefore subject and object are not different substances. The Bodhisattvas realize that nothing whatsoever exists in truth. Whatever may be said to exist does so by virtue of being defined by sets of propositions.

[2] Sambhogakāya.

[3] Nirmāṇakāya.

One, the tendency towards the belief in things as existing in truth is completely overcome, so with the attainment of an immediate and aesthetically vivid awareness these two patterns arise simultaneously without any strain. They always shine together as freely as the sun and its rays.

This is the path common to all those who set out on the highest spiritual course.

(II) The specific division into a starting point, path, and goal is as follows:

The starting point constitutes the three emotively tainted phenomena of birth, death, and the intermediate state.

The path is followed when you make the three existential norms ideally and actually your way of development through a proper knowledge of the methods concerning the Two Stages.

The goal is the effortless realization of the three norms.

When by your efforts you have satisfied your Guru who is well-versed in the methods and full of great compassion, and upon whom depends the whole training course of the Sūtras and Tantras which in its completeness must be born, continue and grow in the disciple's mind; and when you have become fit to receive the initiations, permissions and guidances, then you must at your initiation lay the foundation for the four norms to come to life within you and to dispel all imputations in order to grasp the essence of this experience.

You must keep dearer than your life the commitments and observances which you have taken upon yourself in the presence of the supreme Guru and the deities of the *maṇḍala*.

Since, in particular, your downfall will be all the worse if you give up the Mantric discipline, you have to guard against the fourteen basic transgressions [1] at the risk of your life. You have to be apprehensive and

---

[1] Those who have little or no knowledge of the Buddhist path as it develops from lower to higher levels as a graded process of integration, yet consider themselves as experts entitled to pass judgments, not only claim that the Tantras can be understood without first having studied that which is necessary for their understanding, but also dismiss the disciplinary character of the Tantras. It is important to distinguish between Tantrism as a hard, if not the strictest, discipline, and the Tantrism of those who claim their own fancies to be the substance of Buddhist Tantrism. The reluctance of the *dge-lugs-pa* teachers to propagate Tantric works is based on the sound principle that unless a person is fit to study them he should not be given them. To be fit means not only to be mentally mature but also capable of keeping the commitments and obeying the strict discipline en-

watchful in guarding against the eight gross infractions [1], because they are worse than a violation of the rules of the Prātimokṣa. So you will not be able to avoid any such offences, however much you may try, unless you guard yourself against the chances for transgressions. At the same time you have to take special precautions against the four chances of wrong-doing: ignorance, listlessness, negligence, and giving way to your temper. Therefore you must always heed inspection, meticulousness, self-respect, and decorum.

If the power of these counteragents is weak and that of your emotional states strong, so that you are likely to fail, you must meditate on Vajrasattva [2] in whom the knowledge of all Buddhas is found, purify

---

cumbent on any follower of Tantrism. The fourteen basic transgressions are: (1) to be disrespectful towards the teacher; (2) to overstep the Buddha's words; (3) to be angry with one's co-students; (4) to fail in showing loving-kindness to sentient beings; (5) to forsake an enlightened attitude; (6) to deprecate one's own or others' philosophical views; (7) to divulge that which is secret to those who are not spiritually fit to understand it; (8) to despise one's body-mind which is of the nature of Buddhahood; (9) to have doubts about that which is pure by nature; (10) to pamper evil persons; (11) to have opinions about that which cannot be a content of mind and be given a name; (12) to disgrace those who trust you; (13) not to keep one's commitments; and (14) to despise women whose nature is inspiration.

These fourteen transgressions are a gross disregard of the Three Jewels in which one has taken refuge and, in a sense, are the witnesses of our actions. Transgression no. 1 is directed against the Buddha from whom our teacher is indistinguishable because he imparts knowledge to us and educates us. In proceeding towards our goal we are in need of spiritual friends whom we meet in the community of saintly persons or the Sangha. Transgressions nos. 3 and 12 are directed against true spiritual friends and no. 10 is to succumb to evil friends who lead us astray. The teaching or the Dharma itself is disregarded: in its aspect of revelation by the Buddha by nos. 2, 6, and 7; in its aspect of being a means to realization in so far as the foundation of the path is concerned by nos. 4 and 5; in its two experiences of the First Stage by no. 8 and of the Second Stage by nos. 9 and 11; and in its corollary of making a first start by no. 13 and of finding assistance by no. 14. See *Tskhp* I 11; *Ngbl* IV 2;, 9 seq. *Spl* III.

[1] They are: (1) Wilfully to take a woman who is not suited; (2) to let oneself be influenced by such a woman; (3) not to keep that which is secret from those who are not fit to be told; (4) to quarrel in the presence of saintly persons; (5) to teach something different from the religion in which somebody has faith; (6) to stay for more than seven days with a follower of the Hīnayāna; (7) falsely to boast of psychic faculties; and (8) to teach religion to those who have no faith in it. As to the literature regarding these infractions see the preceding note.

[2] As Tsong-kha-pa in *Tskhp* I 10, 2b points out Vajrasattva is the symbol for the unity of the noetic or the Dharmakāya with the instrumental or the Rūpakāya consisting of the Sambhogakāya and Nirmāṇakāya. See notes 2, 3 and 5, p. 97

yourself of all defilements and mend all broken commitments so making the stream of your cognitions clear and transparent.

You have to accumulate infinite good by making a fourfold offering, an outer, inner, mystic and ultimate one, to the Buddha-sons whom you must imagine as having assembled in the sky at your invitation from the vast Buddha-realms.

Just as a boat without a helmsman cannot cross the ocean, so without the help of Buddhahood manifest and present, the Tantric achievements cannot be effected, and therefore you have to pray intensely to Mañjughoṣa as the patron of your spiritual enterprise, the unique father of all Buddhas, through whose power even the Buddhas of the vast realms have attained their achievements.

The meditation is as follows:

You become conversant with the process of dying and plant the seed for the realization of your highest spiritual norm at the time of winning your goal of Buddhahood, when you meditate on the great radiancy (i. e., of the non-existence of things as entities having an essence by means of which they are what they are) through which the darkness of 'un-knowing' has been dispelled. This is the indivisibility of the pure sphere of no-thing-ness and its cognition in great bliss. This cognition arises after the appearances, in the shape of the stationary and movable, which are like a dense mass of clouds, have been scattered and dissolved in the sphere in which, since beginningless time, there has been no discursive thinking which leads to the belief in things as existing in truth.

You learn about the intermediate state and plant the seed for the realization of authentic communication when you meditate on the idea of Buddhahood as it becomes manifest in a mass of splendour glowing in the richness of its symbols, in the midst of a halo of five resplendent colours, as magnificently as if a mountain of saffron were to fill the sky, the path of the celestials; as if the light of the sun were to fall into an ocean of vermillion; as if the lustre of all the suns in the universe were to gather in a single sun; as if a golden altar were rising higher and higher in the sky; or as this idea transforms itself into the letters of the alphabet conveying the spirituality of all Buddhas who are the lamps of the world, shining in the vast expanse of the sky in a brilliant light of greatest purity; as it fills the sky with its rays of light as if all the suns in the universe had

---

To achieve this unity 'fitness of action' and 'intelligence' must unite. In a certain way, therefore, the meditation on Vajrasattva as a purificatory process is a recapitulation of the whole Buddhist path. See also *Tskhp* III 13a.

become a single sun; as it dispels the spiritual darkness of sentient beings and makes them partake of the nature of ultimate stability; as it satisfies with untainted refreshing flavour the assembly of those who propound Truth [1] in the vast realms; as it gathers everything and turns it into a mass of brilliance; as it emits a five-coloured jewel lustre so intense that all the gems in the world appear as if collected and strung into a precious necklace; or as it reveals its eternal reality in whatever symbolic form in which it may be conceived.

You learn about birth without stains and plant the seed for the realization of an authentic life in the world, when you meditate on the wrathful form [2], terrifying with the unending forms of terror, of Him who (through His awareness which sees directly all that can be known and looks upon sentient beings, infinite as the sky, with compassion) was moved by immense compassion. This was all the greater because He was shocked to see that the crowd of sentient beings in countless impure realms (were firmly fettered by the chains of their actions and emotional states and engulfed in the darkness of spiritual un-knowing so that they) had no chance of hearing the voice of the teaching and of seeing His glorious form so rich in symbols. It is He who shows to the aspirants in their darkness all that is necessary for lifting them out of their predicament and, especially, it is He who appears like a mountain of saffron in celestial space in order to educate the beings of this world and to subdue their deceiver, the belief-in-an-*ens*, as quickly as possible by forcible means. By uttering the syllable *HŪṂ*, which resounds far and wide in a terrifying roar, He frightens all who are poisoned by emotional instability. Out of this indestructible *HŪṂ* in which all the powers of the powerful Buddhas gather, He rises like a mountain resplendent in the colour of lapis lazuli, clad in the garment of the fire that burns when the world comes to an end, wearing the stars and planets as His ornaments, scattering the impure worlds by the breath from his nostrils and burning all the ugliness of Saṃsāra in the flames that leap from the pores of His skin, and in an instant devouring all the three worlds by rolling His tongue like a streak of lightning over His radiant face.

Thus by meditating on the wrathful form of Mañjughoṣa in his palatial mansion, you purify all the stains of the impure worlds and the sentient beings therein and turn them into pure realms and beings. In perfecting

---

[1] The fact that things do not exist in truth as such.

[2] In Tibetan: *rdo-rje 'jigs-byed.*

the four kinds of Buddha-activity (pacificatory, strength-increasing, attracting, and forcible), by using sacred utensils, mantras and concentrations, by speaking sacred formulas and engaging in other spiritually informed activities, and, in particular, by cutting asunder the appetitive web of fetters, the belief-in-an-*ens*, with the sword of discrimination and appreciation, you will quickly attain the highest achievements.

When thus you have ripened all that is positive so that by means of the practice of the First Stage the sublime understanding of the Second or Fulfilment Stage will quickly be born, you must bring about this sublime understanding by immersing yourself in your existentiality after you have prayed intensily to your Guru in divine form whilst practising the unificatory process of the Second Stage.

Only from a competent Guru who is in the spiritual tradition, can you learn this subtle instruction in the Two Stages of the profound path, the essence of the ocean of the Anuttarayogatantra, the secret message of the spiritual heroes and Ḍākas [1] in the three worlds, the sphere more secret than the secret.

May the heroes and Ḍākas of the three worlds always think kindly of me like a mother of her child, and not be angry with me for having shown the door to the Ḍākas' treasures by words which state clearly the secrets of their instruction.

---

[1] Ḍākas are symbols or, to use an expression by Karl Jaspers, 'ciphers of transcendence'. They express the mystery of an existent, of an occurrence, of an affective norm. The Tibetan term, *mkha'-'gro* (also used in the feminine form *mkha'-'gro-ma*, Sanskrit *ḍākinī*) is rendered literally: 'sky-walker'. The Tibetan explanation of the word is that 'sky', 'celestial space' is a term for 'no-thing-ness' and 'to go' means 'to understand'. The Ḍāka or the Ḍākinī is therefore an understanding of no-thing-ness. It is a fine example of 'embodying' language.

CHAPTER SEVEN

THE SPECIFIC GUIDANCE TO THE PROFOUND MIDDLE VIEW OR THE DIRECT MESSAGE OF BLO-BZANG [1]

Praise to Mañjughoṣa!

In heartfelt devotion I praise the Gurus sublime [2]
Who grant all attainments, the highest and the common,
And who, if only to their feet one bows the head,
Wipe out the shortcomings of this world and the next.

Especially I bow to the Teacher beyond compare [3],
The Compassionate Lord, of loving-kindness full
For beings so hard to manage in this evil age
And for the countless host of those who the ten powers possess [4].

In bowing to the great treasure-house of knowledge [5],
Which embodies the spiritual awareness
Of every Buddha in the vast spiritual realms,
I show the mode of being of that which is profound.

---

[1] Short for bLo-bzang grags-pa, Tsong-kha-pa's monastic name. The meaning of this title is that Ye-shes rgyal-mtshan will discuss the 'profound middle view' according to the *dge-lugs-pa* tradition which bases itself through Tsong-kha-pa on the interpretation of the philosophy of Buddhism by Nāgārjuna and Āryadeva.

[2] See note 1, p. 77.

[3] The historical Buddha, Śākyamuni.

[4] The Buddhas. The ten powers are cognitions of (I) what is possible and what not; (II) the relation that holds between one's actions and their results; (III-VI) that which is in volved in he experiences of meditation, liberation, concentration and realization, pertaining to the different intellectual acumen of sentient beings, their different interests and their different psychological backgrounds; (VII) the goals to which the paths lead; (VIII-IX) former lives and future births; and (X) the fact that whatever might arouse emotively toned responses has lost its power to do so.

[5] Mañjughoṣa.

To Tsong-kha-pa I bow down who, through the power
Of his prayers and resolves in former lives,
Combined the Sūtras and Tantras in Tibet
For graded study by the fortunate.

May my whole being be enriched by deeply venerating
The gracious Gurus [1] who point to the unerring path from which
Springs certainty about the real,
Profound and difficult to grasp.

The real purpose of direct instruction which is to be experienced as valuable in this life by those who are fortunate to be human and capable of reasoning, and which is the essence of all Buddha-words and the path travelled by all true sages and saints of yore, has been stated by Nāgārjuna:

Through this good all beings store
Merits and acquire knowledge.
Let them acquire the two true goals
That from knowledge and merits spring.

According to these words it is by making an inner experience of the path complete in its unity of fitness of action and intelligence [2], that the meaning of this purposeful striving reveals itself as goal-attachment, the entrance into the firm citadel of the unity of the two modes, the cognitive-relational and the operational [3]. Here, the infinity of merits is necessary

---

[1] See note 1, p. 77.

[2] See note 2, p. 96.

[3] Dharmakāya and Rūpakāya. The former relates to the noetic nature of man, the latter to his being *with* others and being *in* a world. Dharmakāya and Rūpakāya (the latter consisting of Sambhogakāya and Nirmāṇakāya) have an existential meaning and relate to human existence. These terms, whilst appearing to describe the structure of man, are in fact describing his own existence, though not in a pejorative sense that so easily attaches to the word 'existence', but in the sense of man's act of existing. The more man lives in accordance with these norms or patterns the more his uniqueness is emphasized. The act of existing is most obvious in man's being with others and in the world; it is, however, not something apart from his noetic enterprise. Every noetic act, as the Buddhists have expressed quite clearly, is intentional in structure; and inasmuch as thought and action go together, their proper functioning can be guaranteed only if petty concerns are eliminated and a viewpoint has been found from where one can see and look at things as they really are. Hence the Buddhist demand of disengagement from petty affairs at the beginning, and this must unite with goal-consciousness, (the development of an enlightened attitude) and an unbiased outlook. This outlook, though removed from practical concerns, nevertheless remains intentional in structure and, being removed from the ordinary assumptions and concerns, can unite more

as the cause for the realization of the operational modes [1], just as boundlessness of awareness is a prerequisite for the cognitive-relational one [2]. In this connection the precious enlightened attitude is like the foundation or core of all merits, and the profound 'middle view' [3] is the essential feature of all awareness. Therefore, all the basic and interpretative writings have stated again and again that an enlightened attitude and a middle view have to be practised to form a unity if you want to reach the citadel of Buddhahood. But should either be lacking there is no chance to reach it. For instance, a sprout grows when such factors as soil, water, temperature and seed combine, but not if any one of them is absent. Similarly, regarding Buddhahood, the path to it must be complete in fitness of action and intelligence. Either aspect alone is insufficient for reaching the goal.

Furthermore, the nature of fitness of action and intelligence must be grasped clearly and in the graded process of their practice there must be no errors. If the cause is faulty no proper result can come of it. For instance, you may have heard that a cow gives milk, but do not know from where the milk comes. Certainly you will get none by pulling the cow's horns or tail.

Therefore, the method of developing a precious enlightened attitude is as follows:

First you have to think about the unsatisfactoriness of the world in general and in particular, and, like a swan flying away from a frozen lake, you have to develop a strong sense of disengagement so as to become thoroughly free from the involvements in the multifarious affairs of the world. Then you must feel the content of your thought when you

---

easily with action. The unity of the Dharmakāya and the Sambhogakāya-*cum*-Nirmāṇakāya thus refers to the structure of the noetic capacity and the operations *with* others *in* a situation. Buddhahood is never a static ideal, it is an authentic act of existing. See also *Tskhp* III 16a and its translation in part I, p. 61.

[1] Rūpakāya. See also previous note.

[2] Dharmakāya. See note 3 on the preceding page.

[3] "'Middle' view" (*dbu-ma'i lta-ba*): In the Mahāyānist context the 'middle' view means such more than the mere avoidance of the extreme judgments of eternalism and nihilism. It indicates, rather, the intentional structure of the act of seeing. Literally translated it would have to be rendered 'the seeing of the middle', but such a linguistic translation is, as is the case with most such translations, *prima facie* absurd. 'Middle' is a name for no-thing-ness (*stong-pa-nyid, śūnyatā*) which signifies the fact that things do not exist in truth. Hence, the 'middle view' is, so to say, to be intuitively aware of the fact that there is nothing which could be said to exist in truth.

consider the intolerable misery of all sentient beings in the world, who, in a sense, are your old mother, and you must develop compassion and loving-kindness which are far stronger and deeper than the love a mother has for her only child. The more intense this feeling of compassion becomes the more you forget about yourself and make the great undaunted resolve to deliver all sentient beings from their involvement in Samsara. By the power of this resolve you must, to the best of your ability, develop a strong intention to attain supreme Buddahood for the sake of all sentient beings. This intention must be like that of a merciful leader who in his compassion for the beings of the human world in their desperate plight due to poverty and affliction, sets out in a ship to fetch the Wish-Fulfilling Gem for their sake, not caring for his own body and life. Thus it becomes very important that you strive with all your strength and skill, in all possible ways, to let a precious enlightened attitude grow. As soon as such an attitude develops you become known as a Bodhisattva or a Buddha-son. This attitude is said to be the specific cause of Buddhahood and is likened to a father's seed. As is stated in the *Bodhicaryāvatāra* (I 9):

> The moment an enlightened attitude is born
> The shackles that bind a being to Saṃsāra
> Fall off: he is called a son of Buddha
> And in this world revered by men and gods.

And (III 25)

> In the family of Buddha have I been born
> Today; I have become a Buddha-son.

In the *Gaṇḍavyūha* (p. 494):

> Oh son of a noble family, an enlightened attitude is like the seed of all Buddha qualities. As it makes the good qualities of beings grow it is like a field; as it is a support for the whole world it is like the earth; as it abolishes all poverty it is like Vaiśravaṇa (the god of wealth); as it protects all Bodhisattvas it is like a father; as it grants all desires it is like the Wish-Fulfilling Gem; as it perfects all aspirations it is like an auspicious jar.

And in the *Rājāvavādaka*:

> Your Majesty, you are fully occupied with your many duties, and while you cannot practise the perfections beginning with liberality and ending with an appreciative-discriminative understanding, in each and every way, at least aspire for an enlightened attitude, have faith in it, strive for it, pray for it, and whether you walk, stand, sit, rest, wake up, eat or drink, constantly and always be mindful of it and make it a life-experience. Gather all the roots of the good pertaining to Buddhas, Bodhisattvas, Śrāvakas, Pratyekabuddhas

and ordinary beings, of your own past, future and present, and rejoice in measuring and counting them. The best way to do so is to let this joy attain the highest pitch and become as pervasive as the sky and as intensive as the feeling experienced when one has passed beyond suffering. After that make offerings to all the Buddhas, Bodhisattvas, Śrāvakas and Pratyeka-buddhas. Then do the same to all other beings. Then thrice a day direct this good to unsurpassable, truly perfect enlightenment so that all sentient beings may attain omniscience and all Buddha qualities become perfect. Your Majesty, if you do so, not only will your affairs of state not suffer, but all that pertains to enlightenment will be accomplished. Your Majesty, when your Karma permeated by the good of a truly enlightened attitude ripens you will be born many times among gods and men, and everywhere, be it among gods or men, you will be a ruler. But, Your Majesty, at present it is unknown whether your Karma due to the good of an enlightened attitude is deficient or replete. Anyhow, Your Majesty, by merely attempting an unsurpassable truly enlightened attitude in order to deliver all sentient beings, to free them and to make them breathe freely and to liberate them from suffering, countless and immeasurable foundations of good are accumulated. What more is there to be said and done?

Thus it has been stated repeatedly in many Sūtras, and Tsong-kha-pa said in this connection [1]:

An enlightened attitude is the foundation of the finest road;
The ground and support of far-reaching moral conduct (for which) the two

Accumulations, like that stone of the philosophers,
Are a treasure of virtues in which the highest good is found.
Knowing this, the heroes, the sons of Buddha treasure this precious
Jewel of a mind as the source of true spirituality.

By virtue of being supported by such an attitude, whatever good may have been done, even the most minute, it will not become exhausted but will grow until the goal, Buddhahood, has been reached. But if there is no enlightened attitude, you cannot set out on the Mahāyāna path however much you may busy yourself with contemplative exercises that relate to such topics as structure, motility, and creativity [2]. Rather,

---

[1] *Tskhp* II 2, 66b seq., and commented upon in *Ktsh* 175b seq.

[2] The same has been stated in *Zhdm* 165b.

The meditation topics mentioned (structure (*rtsa, nāḍi*), motility (*rlung, vāyu*) and creativity (*thig-le, bindu* or *tilaka* in Buddhist Sanskrit) are not ends in themselves, rather they are means to overcome the preoccupation with things. Linguistic translations render these operational terms by 'veins', 'vital air' and 'seminal drop'. In so doing they fail to understand the intentional meaning of these highly technical terms. I do not deny that these terms may sometimes mean what the

your good dwindles, as a rule, and often becomes exhausted. But even if this should not be the case there is apart from following the Hīnayāna path no chance of entering the Mahāyāna fold. This is stated in the *Bodhicaryāvatāra* (I 12):

All other good is like a weed,
For when it has born fruit it fades;
But the tree of enlightenment grows slow
And sure and does not wither when it fruits.

In the *Matisāgaraparipṛcchāsūtra*:

Drops of water falling in the ocean
Are not lost as long as the sea remains;
So the good directed to supreme enlightenment
Will not lessen 'til enlightenment is won.

And Nāgārjuna said:

How can you become a Bodhisattva
If you followed the Hīnayāna path
And have not been instructed in his aspiration
Or how he dedicates his conduct (to enlightenment)?

Since this has been expressly stated in many Sūtras and Śāstras, Tsong-kha-pa declared [1]:

---

quantitative language of the physical world points to, but this reduction of technical terms to physical (and physiological) counters overlooks the fact that terms have no meaning in themselves but are noises used by someone to refer to something. Just to look in a dictionary and find that this or that word means this or that is to be naively ignorant of meaning and to be too lazy to find out what was the intention of the person who used the term. As to the systematic ambiguity of the words 'meaning' and 'means', which has caused so much harm to a proper understanding of alien thought, see L. S. Stebbing, *A Modern Introduction to Logic*, Methuen & Co., London 1953, pp. 499 seqq.

A detailed analysis of the import of what is pointed to by 'structure', 'motility', and 'creativity' is given in my *The Life and Teaching of Nāropa*, pp. 149 seqq.

The meditational body-image indicated by the term *rtsa* is radically different from our ordinary body-image; it indicates 'structure' rather than anatomical sections. Similarly, *rlung* relates to the vibrations that pass along the structured paths; it is not identical with breath or breathcontrol which may assist in focusing one's attention on bodily sensations for their exteriorization. Lastly, *thig-le* is rather a feeling of expanding and of seeing in a new light and order, as it is felt when life is pulsating in fullness and freshness; a feeling that can be compared only inadequately with the exultation of the orgasm.

[1] *Tskhp* XIII 172a; XIV 1, 87b.

It is not enough that the religion is Mahāyānist; the individual himself must become a Mahāyānist. Since to be a Mahāyānist depends on an enlightened attitude, your being one is proportionate to your understanding of this attitude. If this attitude is complete in all its aspects, so will be the Mahāyānist. Hence you have to strive for it.

Therefore, according to the statement in the *bKa'-gdams blo-sbyong*, which says that

Two things have to be done in the beginning and the end, it is of the utmost importance to strive to develop a precious enlightened attitude at the very beginning of your spiritual life; and so also the venerable bLo-bzang chos-kyi rgyal-mtshan said [1]:

From now until enlightenment,
Whether you live one year, one month,
But starting now this day or night,
Kill the chance of there arising the major and attendant
States of emotion that the belief-in-an-*ens* has caused;
Again and again remember to devote yourself to practising
The development of two kinds of enlightened attitude,
Their stability and growth by deed, by word, by thought.

That is, as soon as you get up in the morning you should cease completely to be concerned with this life, hold firmly to an enlightened attitude, and remind yourself strongly to do your work, as long as you live, this year, this month, and particularly, these twenty-four hours, in a spirit benefitting sentient beings. At the same time you have to envisage clearly the desire to do everything for the sake of sentient beings, whether you walk, sit, rest or stand. When you do so, the words of the *Samādhirājasūtra* apply:

However much yuo think of Him,
While with Him stay these thoughts, in Him
Rests the mind. And thus you are
Aware of Śākyamuni
Whose qualities of body and of spiritual knowledge
Cannot be measured. When constantly you have practised this,
To it is your mind attuned.
Wheter you sit, stand or rest
For the Buddha-awareness
You yearn, for enlightenment you pray,
Desiring to conquer the whole world.

---

[1] The two kinds of an enlightened attitude are the conventional one of intending to find Buddhahood in order to become a living example to others in their attempt to set out on the path of integration, and the ultimate one of realizing the non-existence in truth of all that is with the coimplicate of its apparitional presence.

And,

Pure in body, speech and mind
He recites the Buddha's names.
By training thus his mind, each day
And night he sees the Lord of the world.
Should he feel ill or despondent,
Or that the pains of death approach
He will not lose sight of the Buddha, he will
Not be overcome by feelings of distress.

There are countless passages to this effect. Since, whether you start from the Sūtras or Tantras, a precious enlightened attitude is the very life of the Mahāyāna path, only an outline of it could be given here. The way to develop and cultivate such an attitude is detailed in the *Byang-chub lam-rim* to which you should refer [1].

The necessity to strive for the awareness of the profound middle view as the true cause for the realization of the ultimate existential norm, is stated by Nāgārjuna:

There is no other way
To freedom but the one
Followed surely by all Buddhas,
Pratyekabuddhas and Śrāvakas.

This is to say that any goal attainable within the three spiritual courses can be reached only by this 'middle view'. And to call the culmination of intelligence 'mother' means that when this profound middle view is practised in unity with an enlightened attitude, it becomes the cause of Buddhahood by proceeding along the Mahāyāna path; but when you practise it through the three disciplines [2], without an enlightened attitude, the Hīnayāna goal is attained. To give an example, when a female cohabits with various males the child born is determined by the status of he who begot it [3]. Therefore the *Mahāyānottaratantraśāstra* (I 34) says:

---

[1] Especially *Tskhp* XIII and XIV are meant.

[2] Aiming at developing ethics and manners, meditational practices and 'intelligence'.

[3] This simile has been taken from *Tskhp* XIII 172b; XIV 1, 88a; and III 8b. The difference between Hīnayāna and Mahāyāna is not determined by a difference in intelligence, the capacity to understand and to appreciate no-thing-ness, although certain statements might be read as intending the Mahāyāna for those of higher intelligence. Intelligence is analytical both in Mahāyāna and Hīnayāna. In both

Aspiration for the highest way is the (causal) seed;
Intelligence is the mother bearing Buddha-qualities.

Here the enlightened attitude is likened to a father's seed and the intelligence which intuits no-thing-ness to the mother [1]. Just as to produce a child a father and mother are both necessary, neither being able to do so alone, so for the birth of Buddhahood both an enlightened attitude and the middle view are necessary, for neither can effect this alone. And so Tsong-kha-pa said [2]:

If by intuition one cannot understand that which Being is,
However much one may withdraw from the world and win enlightenment,
One never will cut off Saṃsāra's root.
Strive then to understand the relative.

What, then, is this profound middle view? It is the intelligence which intuits no-thing-ness or the true existentiality of all that is. And how can this existentiality (be described)? A Sūtra answers:

Deep, peaceful, beyond all judgment, abstract
And radiant – like nectar have I found it.
Even if pointed out none can understand it
Discursively. Where you cannot speak, be silent.

---

courses its objective reference is *śūnyatā*, no-thing-ness. That which is discerned as non-existing is different with the three courses and is determined by the 'enlightened attitude', which distinguishes a 'saintly person' from an ordinary man. For the Śrāvakas it is the non-existence of a Self, be this a Pure Ego or a Central Event; for the Pratyekabuddhas the non-existence of external objects in addition; and for the Mahāyānists (Bodhisattvas) the non-existence in truth of all that is. This goal-consciousness together with the readiness to be there for others is the real differentiating factor.

See *Tskhp* XIV 1, 88b.

[1] In *Tskhp* II 2, 207b seq., Tsong-kha-pa says: "Since the discriminative acumen which immediately apprehends no-thing-ness, like a mother, is the common cause for bringing four sons (i.e., the four philosophical schools of the Vaibhāṣikas, Sautrāntikas, Vijñānavādins and Mādhyamikas) into the world, one speaks of it as 'Mother' (*yum*), and since an enlightened attitude is the specific cause of Buddhahood, it has been many times likened to a father's (*yab*) seed. The reason for calling a man in whose mind that which prevents him from falling into the Hinayana is present, a Buddha-son, is precisely this presence of an enlightened attitude. Hence to the best of one's ability one should try to have such a precious enlightened attitude come about, if it has not yet done so; to have it continue if it has already come about; and to have it develop more and more if it continues. Then it will have to be taken as the starting-point of one's practice. If only lip-service is paid to it the whole Mahāyāna becomes a farce; but if it is something genuine Mahāyāna will be genuine".

[2] *Tskhp* II 2, 231a seqq.

And Nāgārjuna said [1]:

No-thing-ness conceived wrongly
Destroys those with little minds
Like a snake grasped by the tail
Or a spell when wrongly used.
Since the unintelligent
Ever find this teaching hard,
Buddha was reluctant
To divulge it to them.

As, then, the profound existentiality of all that is is difficult to understand, how can people as dull as I be expected to decide that it is this or that? Nevertheless, I will try to explain it a little as I have heard it from my noble Gurus who are in the spiritual tradition.

Candrakīrti once said:

I bow down to him who feels compassion for the beings
Who are as powerless (to act) as a water-mill [2].
Attached to a self by the mere index
'I' they have concretized it as a 'Mine'.

And in his *Pramāṇavarttikā* he said:

If there be an 'I' then there is a 'Thou'
And from the 'I' and 'Thou' come lust and hate,
From the two together
All evil has been born.

It is certain that we beings of the three worlds roam about in Samsara with no independence left, suffering unbearable misery. This fact ultimately is reducible to the deceiver 'Belief-in-an-*ens*', and, therefore it is necessary to find a way to expose him. But as we cannot do this in the way we extract a thorn from our flesh, we have to destroy his sham

---

[1] Mūlamadhyamakakārikā XXIV 11-12.

[2] In *Tskhp* XVI 1, 13ab six reasons are given for comparing man's life with a water-mill: (1) men are tightly fettered by their karmic acts and emotional upsets; (2) they are urged on by consciousness which is like the man operating the water-mill; (3) without interruption they go up and down in the well of Saṃsāra; (4) without efforts on their part they fall into evil forms of life, but it is hard work to be pulled up to higher forms; (5) although the chain of interdependent origination can be divided into three sections relating to emotional dispositions, karmic acts, and emotively toned responses, it is impossible to say where the one ends and the other begins; and (6) every day man's life becomes disordered by three types of misery. – Considering these three types of misery see note 3, p. 83.

fortress by recognizing the faultiness of this straying into bad thinking and dismantle its stronghold by finding genuine certainty about reality. This is done thus:

If you are afraid that there is a scorpion in your house you do not feel at ease until this fear has been removed and so you have to do something to dispel it. However, you cannot do so merely by thinking that there is no scorpion in the house. You have to search all the nooks and corners with your eyes wide open and when you have convinced yourself that there really is no scorpion, your former apprehensiveness and terror are overcome. This simile points out that the belief-in-an-*ens*, our ego, has to be refuted because from beginningless time until now our mind, which has been taken in by and desires the phenomenon of the 'I' as something true with regard to our psycho-physical constituents, has brought us misery. However, this belief is not refuted by sitting idle and stopping all discursive reasoning by not thinking at all. You must become certain that an 'I' does not exist in truth as a separate entity. It cannot be denied that even in our dreams we are clearly aware of ourselves as 'I', 'I'. If, however, we investigate this phenomenon of dreaming we find that the fact of the 'I', as being true in connection with the psycho-physical constituents, appears to be an established fact, and not a projection of this wandering of the mind. Having been taken in by and wanting this phenomenon, the mind is hopelessly bewildered through the 'belief-in-an-*ens*' or 'I'. If the 'I' in this process of appearing is with the psycho-physical constituents, we must ask ourselves whether our body or our mind is this 'I' or whether it exists apart from them.

If the body is the 'I', it should end when the body is cremated after death. (This is not the case, as each new existence is tied up with the 'I') [1], hence the body is not the 'I'.

If the mind is the 'I', I should not be susceptible to ailments, burns and wounds, because mind is not something that can be set afire or be burnt to cinders. But this is contrary to common experience. Furthermore, it would be meaningless to say: 'my mind', just as it is nonsense to say: 'the I of the I'. When I say 'my mind' I have the idea that 'I' am the owner and the 'mind' is my property. If the mind were the 'I' this

---

[1] In *Tskhp* XVIII 7, 4b, Tsong-kha-pa declares that if one holds to the view that the 'I' ends with the cremation of the body, then the axiom of life continuing through various forms would be meaningless. The same statement is found in *Khg* X 3, 3b. That the axiom of repeated existences does not necessarily imply the existence of an 'I' or 'Pure Ego' is clearly stated in *Zhdm* 201b.

could never happen. To illustrate this point: when you say 'the ornaments of a woman', the woman appears to be the owner and the ornaments her property. It is meaningless to say that the woman is the ornaments.

If the 'I' exists apart from the body and mind, it ought to be demonstrable as this or that after the body and mind have been separated. Since this is not the case, the 'I' does not exist apart from the body and mind.

When, in spite of your search, you have been unable to find an 'I', you have become absolutely certain that an 'I' does not exist in truth as such, by itself apart from being used as an index with which to label the psycho-physical constituents. This is called the 'profound middle view'.

It is possible to think of many other similes to illustrate this point and so there are a great many ways to bring this certainty about. Since my Gurus, the lords of saintly sages, have said that there are many other means to overcome this belief-in-an-*ens* or ego, a few similes may be given:

(I) If you travel over a wide plain and see three scarecrows in the distance you may have the illusion of these scarecrows being three men. This illusion does not manifest itself as a projection of your mind but as the perception of some persons in the distance. If, moreover, they appear to move about you become afraid that they are robbers or take them for fellow-travellers. When you have come nearer and look them over properly you see that they are but stones and heaps of straw, and you become thoroughly convinced that they are not men. Similarly, although for us the 'I', mountains, fences, palaces, and houses appear to be true as real objects, by the instruction of a Guru we become convinced that if we search with clear reason we find that nothing exists in truth except the set of postulates in use.

(II) When horses, oxen, and other natural things appear in our dreams, not knowing them to be created by our minds, we believe that they are there as real objects and we experience a variety of joys and sorrows, affections and aversions. If we examine this when we wake up we become convinced that there have never been any horses or oxen apart from the fact of our dreaming. Similarly the idea of an 'I' and 'he' or 'she', 'friend' and 'enemy', are but manifestations of our own ignorant erring minds, and we should become accustomed to think that there is not a single entity existing in truth as such.

(III) When in the twilight we walk along a road and see a dusty rope we may have the illusion of a snake, and since this illusion does not manifest as a projected creation of our mind but as if a snake were coming toward us as a real object, we feel terrified and worried; but if in order to dispel this fright we take a lamp and investigate with our eyes open, we see that what frightened us is but a dusty rope and we become convinced that apart from the illusion there is no snake at all. In the same way we have the idea of an 'I' or of our body, this idea does not come as a postulate but as a solid objective fact. On account of this we develop love and hate towards that which seems to be acceptable or unacceptable; through love and hate we accumulate Karma and through the power of Karma we wander about in Saṃsāra with no independence left, and experience many sorts of misery. When you have investigated this matter with the help of a Guru's instruction and have become convinced that the 'I' apart from being a postulate or index does not exist as it seems to do, you still must think further about it.

In order to corroborate this matter so as to help the development of this certainty the following quotations will serve. It is stated in the *Aṣṭasāhasrikā*:

> The belief in an 'I' and a 'Mine' makes sentient beings roam in Saṃsāra.

In the commentary of the *Catuḥśataka*:

> It is certain that 'existence' due to a positive fiction and 'non-existence' due to a negative one do not exist as such by virtue of an essence through which they are what they are, but only like a coiled rope labelled a snake.

In the *Lam-rim chen-mo* [1]:

> That which exists as a substantival constituent or an essence without having been posite by a mind, is called 'ontological status' or 'being-itself'. Its non-existence with regard to the specific reference 'individual' is called 'the non-existence of a self as an absolute principle', and regarding such references as eyes, ears and other physical constituents, it is considered as 'the non-existence of the entities of reality as absolute principles'. The belief in such 'being-itself' existing with reference to any thing can easily be understood as the belief in the two forms of an *ens* (psychological and physical).

The great rGyal-ba dbEn-sa-pa declared:

> The immediate appearance of an 'I' as agent is the perverse appearance-process of this very phenomenon. Since it is found with all beings of the world it is called the 'co-mergent belief' in existence being true in itself. It is also belief in something entitatively absolute as well as a belief-in-an-*ens*. It is referred to by the term 'that which is to be refuted'.

---

[1] *Tskhp* XIII 397b.

Further, he said:

Oral precept is the Guru's direct instruction about the proper procedure which leads to the experience of what is meant by the scriptures instead of letting oneself be fettered by their wording. When you have become acquainted thoroughly with all that has been explained previously, you should take up the meditation posture called the 'seven points' as described in the *rNam-snang* [1], and relax your mind in a condition where no projective postulations occur. When in this state if you watch how the projective-postulational activity sets in when the idea of the 'I' has risen, you (will realize) how the terms self-evidence, factuality, being-itself, and other labels have been used in connection with the appearance of the 'I' as a self-evident and factual object before the mind.

And,

If you investigate existentiality or the being-itself of all phenomena linked up with the belief-in-an-*ens* and the (attendant) belief in a 'Mine', they turn out to possess no criteria for existence in truth and as such because they are void of a truth-principle, and so are like empty space. For instance, white, black, and other kinds of clouds appear in the sky and, in the end, not being something permanent, they vanish. In other words the truth-nothingness of clouds is void of any truth-principle. Similarly, all common appearances due to this belief in a self and in a 'Mine' disappear upon investigation and are like empty space, being nothing (in themselves) and yet true without being something that exists in thruth. Just as clouds gather by chance, so all the entities of Saṃsāra and Nirvana, the belief-in-an-*ens* and in a 'Mine' are like an apparition, appearing under specific conditions but being nothing as such.

Further,

For us beings of the world all external things do not exist in truth by themselves apart from being postulated as existing. When we become aware of them they seem to exist in truth by themselves, and we, according to this apparent mode, develop an unfortunate love for ourselves and hatred for others and other sundry emotions, and experience various kinds of misery through them in Saṃsāra. How is this non-existence in truth of things to be demonstrated? Four logical procedures [2] apply here: the certainty of the ap-

---

[1] This is the *Vairocanābhisambodhitantra* in which the postures of the body for fruitful meditation are discussed, such as sitting cross-legged, straight and so on.

[2] Meditation as a means towards goal-achievement must be done with the help of 'intelligence' and not by merely staring empty-minded into empty space. 'Intelligence', which in the Buddhist sense of the word always relates to man's existence and not to solving tasks the solution of which is already at hand, works best when properly trained by 'logic'. Unfortunately the term 'logic' is likely to raise a serious misunderstanding because it is almost exclusively understood to refer to a mathematical ('symbolic') treatment of a subject matter. 'Logic' in

pearance of that which can and is to be refuted; the certainty of the principle of entailment; and the certainty of the principles of neither singularity nor plurality. Through these four principles certainty about the non-existence of any thing in truth is achieved. The first principle states: When you have relaxed your mind in a condition of peace and tranquillity so that no projective postulations occur, cognition clears, becomes radiant and translucent. Out of this condition of peace the idea of the 'I' may rise by itself or it may be made to rise. At the same time as this idea stirs, the mode of its arising must be understood.

The venerable bLo-bzang chos-kyi rgyal-mtshan said:

Whatever appears for us ordinary beings as the manifestations of Saṃsāra and Nirvana with its 'I' and so on does so as if it were independent, inasmuch as it is a self-evident objective reference. The belief that it exists as it appears is precisely that which has to be refuted. When you are certain of this you have to think that whatever appears in general and as an object before the mind in particular, appears so in relation to many factors. The essence of any instruction is the preservation of the continuity of this conviction by intelligent inspection which reveals that appearance and appetance do not exist in truth.

And in the *dGa'-ldan bka'-brgyud rin-po-che'i bka'-srol phyag-chen yang-gsal sgron-me* we read:

For us, when we are not subject to the naive belief in things, all entities should appear merely as postulates or names. That this is not the case is due to the deceptive activity of the demon 'Un-knowing' through which the existentiality (of that which is nothing as such) appears in the perverted form (of being something as such) and through addiction to this perversion we accumulate Karma. Through the power of Karma we roam about in Saṃsāra and suffer all sorts of misery. To put things bluntly: This mode of appearance and of appetance is called the appearance of that which is refutable or the appearance of something existing in truth, and the belief in things as existing in truth or appetance respectively.

Buddhism is an instrument of knowledge and its adequacy is appraised in terms of the real which is known through this instrument. The difference in meaning of the word 'logic' in Buddhism and in modern Western philosophy lies in the fact that in Buddhist logic the discipline is adapted to its subject matter, while in modern mathematical logic the subject matter is subordinated to the tool. See the trenchant critique by Henry Babcook Veatch, *Intentional Logic*, New Haven. Yale University Press. 1952, *passim*.

The four logical procedures outlined in the text can only be applied when the state of tranquillity has been achieved, because tranquillity facilitates 'insight' and 'logical' investigation. See *Ktsh* 187b; *Khg* VII 11, 2b.

From the *lTa-ba'i nyams-mgur*:

When the mind has been disturbed by the demon 'Belief-in-Things'
It postulates perversions and then becomes involved in them.
Through this power you differentiate between the self and others,
Through Karma and emotive states you wander in Saṃsāra.
If the foe 'Belief-in-an-*ens*' is not deprived of life
By the sharp sword 'Understanding-essentiality',
In this ocean of the world in which it is so hard
To live, this great round of misery will never end.

And,

When you look into the face of what appears to be
You will know it to be unstable and deceptive.
When you cognize it, truth's face is revealed: the mind
Stands naked of its veils deprived, – nothing as such.
All acts, whether pure or defiling, indivisibly do
Blend together in the sphere of ultimate reality.
The path free from assertion and negation winds on as good
And evil to be done or shunned by a discerning mind.

And,

If the enchanter 'Belief-in-an-*ens*' has entered once
Your heart, you overestimate yourself without restraint
As to your status, you are (at once) tormented by
Those devilish views, eternalism and nihilism;
You are afflicted by diseases, the fevers and chills of love and hate;
You suffer from blood-streaked diarrhoea and vomit all your evil deeds.
Again and again life frustrated is in higher forms
And a vast mass of suffering met with in the world.
In view of this your tears should flow, despondent,
To be pitied, you should take fright and recoil.
But when you see what is as such,
Laugh, be happy and contented.

And,

From the time without beginning until now
This demon has (long) dwelt within my heart:
That which has no self for self has been taken.
Deluded by the guiles of a quick profit
For times that are countless I have burned in hell.
Today through the Guru's favour I have seen
The real nature of mind, beyond assertions.
Now that I have seen the lure of 'Belief-in-an-I', that foe
And that enchanter, the young groom called 'Cognition Self-arisen'
And the sweet bride 'Reality' have met in radiant bliss.

The marriage of appreciation and cognition, blending with blissful
awareness and the real
That can be known, is the glorious friendship that need not be
consummated and never can be split.

And,

I looked at all beings and all realms as friends
And when I thought of all their being, my mind
Became intoxicated by the wine of 'Belief-Things'.
I tired of winnowing the chaff, of the non-existence
Of deeds and effects, but when I saw they were related
I rejoiced and felt compassionate in this round of forms.
Those whom the demon 'Belief-in-an-I' ensnares
May well believe in what appears as really true.
But when reason and revelation clear the mind
And the eye discerns the Real, you see the object
Of your desires brought like a flower in the sky
By that great enchanter 'Belief-in-an-*ens*'.
Having twisted the truth of an 'I' into truth absolute,
This old heap that is myself, causing so much regret,
Today has vanished into the sphere of no-thing-ness.

If you are certain about existentiality in the sense that an 'I' or self does not exist in truth, all the other entities of reality are easily understood to be of the same nature by the same logic, and certainty about the real existentiality of all that is is quickly won. As is stated in the *Samādhirājasūtra*:

When you know the 'I'
Try all else to know.
That which all things are
Like the sky is pure.
All is known through one,
By one all are seen.
When one thing is seen

Āryadeva said:

So is all the rest.
The no-thing-ness of one
Is no-thing-ness of all.

Against this the objection might be raised that if all things are mere fictions they do not exist at all. This is not the case: I and all the other entities exist, but not as they appear to do through the bewildering workings of the mind. How then do they exist? They exist only in so far as they are names, indexes, and labels. For instance, when different pieces of wood are joined together in a certain way we speak of a cart and by this label the cart is said to exist and thereby exerts its efficacy. Similarly the combination of a body and a mind is given the label 'I' or 'self' and only in this respect does the 'I' exist, capable of accumulating Karma and experiencing joys and sorrows as its result. This allocation of Karma and its result to a mere label is very difficult to understand and as long as you are not clear about it you have not won the 'middle view'. Such are the words of my venerable Gurus. This also is what the Buddha wanted to convey, as explained by Nāgārjuna and his disciples, and this unquestionably is what Tsong-kha-pa and his disciples mean.

The *Anavataptaparipṛcchāsūtra* states:

> That by conditions caused has never come about,
> For in it nothing comes about by being this.
> All that depends on conditions is nothing.

Nāgārjuna declared:

> Origin through relations is
> The Buddha's rich, profound treasure.

Candrakīrti asserted:

> Since things are caused by that to which they are related,
> Their presence does not stand investigation.
> This logic inherent in the relative
> Destroys countless webs of erroneous views.

Tsong-kha-pa himself declared [1]:

> It is not difficult to understand, when one critically examines the matter, that there is nothing which lasts as an object existing through a principle by which it is what it is, and that everything appears by way of relations is merely ephemeral like mist. The real difficulty, since the above features apply to the smallest items which have been revealed by the Mādhyamika philosophy to be non-existent as being-itself, is to abolish this (assumption of a) being-itself in all its ramifications, and to have this certainty that the individual, who is nothing in himself, is the perpetrator of acts and the receiver of their results. Since these two features, non-existence in truth and apparitional existence, are rarely realized, the middle view is so difficult to win.

---

[1] *Tskhp* XIV 1, 183a seq.

And [1],

All the frailties of the world
Are rooted (deep) in ignorance:
That which destroys all when seen
Relativity is called.
How can a thinker
Not become convinced
About the most important truth that you have taught:
The path of relational origination?
If so, when praising you, the Lord,
Who will not feel
Of wonder full
About relativity?
What deeper and more wondrous ways
Are there but to say: whatever
Depends upon conditions
Is void of any being?

And [2],

He who sees that all things in Saṃsāra and Nirvana
Are infallible in their cause and in their effect
And in whom all preconceived ideas have vanished,
Has set out down the path in which all Buddhas delight.
As long as the twin ideas of appearance, infallible in the relative,
And of no-thing-ness that cannot be described, are separate,
the Buddha's message
Has not been understood. But when certainty
In which there is no belief in things prevails,
By seeing all at once and not alternately
That relativity is most infallible,
The philosophical search comes now to an end.

The venerable bLo-bzang chos-kyi rgyal-mtshan said:

By looking at the things of Saṃsāra and Nirvana
One sees that the cause-effect relation
Is most infallible and subtle.
Like a rainbow in the sky where walk
Immortals, appearance and no-thing-ness are not an alteration:
The sphere, pure and free at first from straying into the belief in truth
And the relation between cause and effect are infallible.

---

[1] *Tskhp* II 2, 15a seq.
[2] *Ibid.*, 231b seq. See also *Ktsh* 17b.

The middle path of unity knows, indeed, no bounds.
Through your favour I have found
This path, you second Buddha.

And,

Things by name are devoid of truth, but in a game
Of cause and effect appear as truth and naught.
By the Guru's favour (alone) is found the path
Where no-thing-ness and cause-effect united lie.
Ah, from dangers of eternalism and nihilism is this path free.

And,

In Saṃsāra and Nirvana
There are no things except
This game of naming them and so
We have no fear of birth and death.
When never finding rest I used to roam, but now have reached
The home of peace, no-thing-ness and ambrosial nectar.
When I think of this I see
My gracious Guru's work.
A son in spirit of the second Buddha,
I sing this song of Seeing Truth, I amuse
Myself on the path with Mahāmudrā.
If you want freedom, do the same, my friends.

And,

When I looked at all things as
Appearances deceptive
They could not withstand my scrutiny
And thus revealed their double nature.
Although I never doubted this profound being
When I heard the words
'The world has crumbled',
This resounding cry made my mind most happy.

And,

Out of a play that has no being in itself, appeared
A many-coloured picture of all the good and evil.
In Saṃsāra and Nirvana
I have seen nothing that was not
A mere postulate or label.

And,

In Saṃsāra and Nirvana be not caught by the appearances
Of things, but look at them in all their existentiality.
If you can see the nature of appearance and no-thing-ness,
From eternalism and nihilism will you be free. I have

Found satisfaction in serving the venerable one who was well
Qualified so that the continuance of his favour did not fail.
Thus the support by Sūtras and Tantras became stronger
And the importance of instruction (far) more rapturous.
If through your good fortune you seek liberation,
Look in the face of reality and put your trust
In the famous Guru for whom
Dry prattle is not scholarship
And a life of uneducated practice is not
Worth the name. Extend far your learning and your studies.

If you have become convinced about no-thing-ness through trustworthy revelation and clear reasoning, the actual practice of it derives from the oral instruction. Having first become attracted by the profound path, the union with the Guru, you should bring your body into the proper posture for meditation and develop this certainty through both discursive and intuitive contemplation. My revered Gurus have said that intuition alone is not sufficient.

It has been said that this profound middle view is the very life of the path outlined in the Sūtras and Tantras, and that in particular the highest Tantras cannot be pursued without this view being present. Therefore, in order to acquire this middle view you first have to remove the blemishes of your karmic actions by making four powerful confessional and expiatory vows [1] and by praying fervently whilst conceiving your Guru and the lordly Mañjughoṣa as indivisible by nature. Then you must strive to pile up merits and acquire knowledge by a seven-point ritual [2] including the offering of a *maṇḍala*, and must purify your actions and observe that to which you have committed yourself. Not only is this of greatest importance, it has also been stated that it is of particular value to recite the profound Sūtras that reveal the direct

---

[1] See note 1, p. 82.

[2] The seven features are: (1) saluting the Guru with folded hands; (2) worshipping him; (3) confessing whatever evil one has done; (4) rejoicing in the good done by others; (5) requesting the Buddhas in all the regions of the world to turn the 'Wheel of the Dharma' (i.e., to proclaim their message); (6) begging them to stay on in the world and not to pass into Nirvana; and (7) directing everything good one has done to the realization of enlightenment.

The preparation of a *maṇḍala* is an elaborate procedure. The *maṇḍala* represents the whole universe, not only in its physical aspect but also as a psychological attitude. The *maṇḍalas* found on Tibetan painted scrolls are, so to speak, the blueprint of the mansion in which the god of one's contemplation lives and of the world in which one sees everything, including oneself, in a light of transfiguration.

meaning of the Buddha's word and thus create a disposition for the middle view to grow, by reading them again and again. To this effect the *Samādhirājasūtra* may serve:

Know all things to be like this:
A mirage, a cloud castle,
A dream, an apparition,
Without essence but with qualities that can be seen.

Know all things to be like this:
As the moon in a bright sky
In some clear lake reflected,
Though to that lake the moon has never moved.

Know all things to be like this:
As people who have gone (alone) to mountain solitudes
Or forests hear the echo of laughter, songs and weeping,
But see not nor hear a thing.

Know all things to be like this:
As an echo that derives
From music, sounds and weeping,
Yet in that echo is no melody.

Know all things to be like this:
Just as you a dream enjoy
But when you wake see nothing,
Only fools will yearn and hanker for this pleasure.

Know all things to be like this:
As a magician makes illusions
Of horses, oxen, carts and other things,
Nothing is as it appears.

Know all things to be like this:
A young woman in a dream
May see her son both born and dead. Yet when he dies
She is sad, while at his birth she was overjoyed.

Know all things to be like this:
As at (mid)night the bright moon
Appears in water crystal-clear, yet
There is no moon and grasped it cannot be.

Know all things to be like this:
At noon in midsummer
A man by thirst tormented, marching on,
Sees a mirage as a pool of water.

Know all things to be like this:
If in a mirage there's no water

Only fools will want to drink it,
For it never can be drunk.

Know all things to be like this:
If you split weeds to find their marrow,
You will always fail. In the same way
Within and without is nothing.

While here only an outline has been given in order to show how necessary it is to learn the union of fitness of action with intelligence and how this can be done, a more detailed account is found in the precious writings of Tsong-kha-pa and his disciples, in the instruction manuals for the enlightenment path, in the basic works of the *dGa'-ldan Mahāmudrā* [1] dealing with the ultimate in instruction and in the commentary on it [2].

To sum up:

I have written down the essence of what my Gurus taught,
It contains the core of all the Sūtras and all Tantras,
Of sages sublime and nobles it is the essence spiritual,
The best entrance for the fortunate who deliverance desire.
I heard it from my Gurus, a treasured gem transmitted
By oral teaching from Tsong-kha-pa, that second Buddha,
From rGyal-ba dbEn-sa-pa, that saint of the great Snow Mountains.
If I have omitted something or said something that is wrong,
Though I have studied much, have reasoned clearly, and have followed
Revelation that can be trusted, may all others
Who have spiritual vision correct all my mistakes.
How can one with little sense like me,
Of all simpletons the simplest, know
The meaning deep and hard to fathom –
A fool's attempt the sky to measure?
If something good be written here,
As wise and saintly Gurus wrote,
Let discerning people judge and say:
'This man has not disgraced the Teaching'.
For this good deed and for all beings' sake
May omniscience be won by all
When, after many (future) lives encouraged by my friends, I shall
Have travelled to its end that auspicious path uniting

---

[1] This is the *dge-ldan bka'-brgyud rin-po-che'i phyag-chen rtsa brgyal-ba'i gzhung-lam* by bLo-bzang chos-kyi rgyal-mtshan (1567-1662 A.D.) together with the author's own commentary, the *dge-ldan bka'-brgyud rin-po-che'i bka'-srol phyag-rgya chen-po'i rtsa-ba rgyas-par bshad-pa yang-gsal sgron-me*.

[2] This is the *dga'-ldan phyag-rgya chen-po'i khrid-yig lam-bzang gsal-ba'i sgron-me* by Ye-shes rgyal-mtshan.

Fitness of action and intelligence. May I become
The foremost leader to liberate all those in the endless
Dread ocean of Saṃsāra swept on by currents turbulent,
By birth, illness, old age and death, to be drowned (at last)
By their larmic acts, by storms by their emotions raised.
May the thousand-rayed sun of Mañjughoṣa's teaching,
The eye that sees and shows the path to countless beings,
Shine for ever in the sphere of Buddha's doctrine
And then open wide the lotus minds of beings.

CHAPTER EIGHT

THE SECRET MANUAL REVEALING THE INNERMOST NATURE OF SEEING REALITY OR THE SOURCE OF ALL ATTAINMENTS

From the depth of my heart I bow with folded hands to and take refuge in the venerable Gurus of unbounded compassion, the great saint dbEn-sa-pa and his disciples as well as in their spiritual succession.

I pray that I may be supported at all times by those who are full of love and compassion and that by their favour I may quickly become spiritually mature and free.

At this moment, when we have found a human life with its advantages and opportunities for enlightenment, so hard to find and so significant when found, the best means to make life worth-while is to exert ourselves by action suited to the winning of supreme enlightenment where all emotional states within us as well as their latent potentialities have been completely eradicated. Moreover, it has been said that this world with its three spheres [1] does not pass beyond a state of unsatisfactoriness and misery which is like tortures experienced when one falls naked into a pit of flames; and that whatever appears now as bliss is but a fancy about it, because some previous unhappiness has subsided for the moment, and actually is not bliss. Therefore, unless we are able to conquer the emotional upsets they will dominate, and whatever we do will be dictated by them. Having come under the power of karmic acts and emotional states there is no independence left to us, and transitoriness is revealed in the momentary changes so that a person's mind is unable to find stability. Since to roam about powerless in Saṃsāra is the ultimate nature of

---

[1] See note 1, p. 83.

misery, we will be able to understand that Saṃsāra is just misery when we start thinking as indicated above.

The root of all misery in the world is the emotionally upsetting unrest within us, and its root is the belief-in-an-*ens*. This belief takes an appetitive object [1], though actually not existing, as existent and thereby becomes completely mixed up with it. As a matter of fact, since beginningless time our mind has fallen a prey to this straying mode of un-knowing and has developed the idea of an 'I' about the affect-arousing constituents of our being, be they single or assembled. Even in our dreams we have this idea of 'I', 'I'. It is therefore imperative to understand how, in thinking of the assemblage of the affect-arousing constituents as an 'I' due to the straying mode of our mind, this phenomenon of existing as such regarding the constituents has come about.

Let us take an example. When at night by the light of a lamp we see the shadow of some sweepings we may have the illusion of a scorpion moving about and feel frightened. When we then examine the phenomenon we find that we do not feel that this is a creation of our mind [2], but that a fearful insect actually is moving towards us. When we cannot get rid of this illusion terror strikes us and unhappiness arises. Similarly, it has been said, through the power of karmic acts the idea of an 'I' regarding the affect-arousing constituents in their totality, though being a creation and projection of our mind, does not appear as such a creation but as if the 'I' comes from the constituents, plain and simple. Due to this illusion we develop various emotions such as love for ourselves and hatred towards others. Through these emotions we perform various actions and it is because of them we roam about in Saṃsāra with no independence left

---

[1] Buddhism distinguishes between pure sensation, a situation where a certain *sensum* such as a coloured patch or a noise is intuitively apprehended but where there is no external reference, and an ordinary perceptual situation where, together with the intuitive apprehension of a *sensum*, certain emotions and feelings of expectation ('appetites') are excited, all of which enter into a specific kind of relation which gives the situation its external reference. C.D. Broad, *The Mind and its Place in Nature*, p. 215 speaks in this connection of the "quasi-Belief about the Sensum". The Buddhists call it an 'appetitive objective situation' where our expectations and our appetance combine.

[2] 'Creation', here, does not mean that something new (not existing before) is being projected, but that there is a cognitive union with the object that exists already which assimilates and reveals it as it already is but in the light of expectations. This peculiar process which does not happen in pure sensation, is described as 'the straying of the mind into the belief of things as existing in truth'. It is a deviation from that which is given actually.

to us and experience all sorts of misery. Thus, on the one hand, we must understand what is meant by the statement that in order to dispel this illusion or belief in a self, there must be an unbiased viewpoint and meditative practice, and on the other, we must remember the dictum that such an unbiased pure mode of seeing does not come about without smashing our emotions.

The method of dispelling this illusion is similar to the one given in the example above. When at night we have the illusion that there is a scorpion while there actually is none, and when with the help of a very bright lamp we search with our eyes open in order to see whether there is a scorpion or not, and when we have become certain that there is none, we are convinced that apart from the process of appearing due to un-knowing there is really nothing whatsoever. By that time all the fears due to an illusion and all their attendant misery subside and become quiet by themselves. Similarly when, with the eye of knowledge aided by the light of the Guru's instruction, we investigate the illusion of the 'I', permeating the affect-arousing constituents of our being, we become certain that there is nothing as it appears and we are convinced that apart from the process of appearing due to un-knowing at that time there is actually nothing so to appear. This conviction is called the 'profound middle view'. When we have this outlook, all actions and emotive states such as love and hate instigated by this illusion of the belief in an 'I' as well as the misery generated by them, subside. While a man of keen intellect and with a previous disposition to such an outlook will gain it merely by recognizing this belief in an 'I' for what it is and as the root of Saṃsāra, the logical refutation is as follows:

If this 'I' as conceived by a mind concerned with the 'I', 'I' exists with regard to the constituents of our being, it must be either identical with or different from them. There is no other alternative. If this 'I' is identical with the constituents it must be terminable because the constituents having come from father and mother are finally discarded at death. This mere 'I', however, has been interminable since beginningless time. The mind being concerned with the 'I' has continued to associate with a body since beginningless time due to the power of karmic acts. Having left one body it has taken up other ones. Since it has taken that body to be the 'I' it has through the power of this illusion taken each combination of the affect-arousing constituents as the 'I' and has roamed about in Saṃsāra. Hence it is certain that the 'I' is not identical with the constituents. On the other hand, if the 'I' as it appears as 'I' is assumed to be different from the constituents, this cannot be the case because if it existed apart from them it ought to be pointed out as 'this is the I' and, when the body is touched by fire and we have the feeling which we express by saying 'I feel the heat', then, if the 'I' and the body were different from each other there would be no necessity for the 'I' to be affected when the body is touched. For instance, since a pillar and a jug are two different things, the jug is not automatically touched when the pillar is. It is therefore an established fact that the 'I' as it appears in the belief in an 'I' is not something apart from the body. When we are thus certain that the 'I' is neither identical with nor different from the psycho-physical constituents we develop the firm conviction that apart from the process of appearing there is no entity whatsoever existing in truth.

Further, when a person suffering from jaundice sees a white conch as yellow, it is safe to say that the yellow is not in the conch but merely appears to be there due to the patient's affected vision. So, while due to our affliction by un-knowing we have the idea of an 'I' with regard to the psycho-physical constituents, we can be fully convinced and certain that there actually is nothing existing so in truth.

Also in the case of other individuals the assemblage of a physical aspect, the flesh and the bones derived from the fertilizing and materiality-producing forces of father and mother, and a mental aspect, consciousness, appear in various guises such as a human being, a donkey or a horse and so on, and we take it for granted that such and such an aggregate of aspects is a man or an animal without having the idea that this is but a projected creation of our mind's working. Since various emotions, such as love and hate, arise within us with reference to those aggregates and since karmic acts are accumulated and performed through them, this root of all appearance processes straying into the belief in concrete existence, must be eradicated inasmuch as it is the cause of all misery.

While we believe our projections to exist in truth, thinking that a certain aggregate of conditions is a man or taking a shadow of some sweepings as a scorpion or a distant scarecrow as a man, we must develop certainty by knowing that actually there is nothing existing in truth.

In short, whatever comes before our senses does not exist in truth but appears to do so and is like a magic show; any assumption of that which is not something to be something is a form of bluff; the non-existence of any essence is like a bubble; and the stray appearances due to sundry causes and conditions are like an echo. Again and again we have to develop this certainty by clearly and decidedly thinking that whatever appears now does not exist in truth. To put it concisely once more, we have to win the certain knowlegde that there exists nothing in truth apart from all appearances being but a projection and creation by our mind.

When we have won this certain knowledge that, although not existing in truth, the appearance of pleasure and sorrow, of good and evil, is due to various conditions such as karmic acts and emotional states, we can attempt the path which unites fitness of action and intelligence by relying on the fact that appearance and no-thing-ness are mutually compatible. To consolidate this conviction that by following this path the goal or the unity of the two patterns [1] will be achieved, is the very essence of practising the 'middle view' [2].

Further, when we have convinced ourselves that whenever this idea of an 'I' arises regarding the psycho-physical constituents there is no reason to believe in them as an 'I' and to overevaluate them because this body, having been derived from father and mother, in the end will be discarded, we should settle our mind in a condition of seeing the existentiality of all that is. We should think that the virulent poison of hatred becomes utterly ineffective and in a moment turns into enlightenment when, by dismissing our preoccupations with the body from our mind and turning then over to countless demons and evil spirits, these obnoxious elements merely smell and taste the blood and flesh while eagerly devouring it. Then we should become composed in a condition which is like the empty sky with nothing to be perceived because this mass of flesh and blood of our body has been eliminated. And when we arise out of this composure we should try to understand all that appears as delusive and errant. My Gurus have said that even if we think so once in a while, it needs great effort actually to repel the attack of evil spirits and in addition to destroy the belief in an 'I'.

When demoniac forces such as illness and others afflict the body we should utter the mantra *phaṭ* and dismiss the idea of our body from our mind as if it had turned rotten. Our mind which then assumes the radiant and bliss-saturated form of Heruka, turns into an ocean of nectar when by the mantra *oṃ āḥ hūṃ* the material body consisting of flesh and blood has been eliminated. By making this nectar available to all persons, ordinary and saintly, they will be honored by this oblation. Then we should think that at that very moment the beings of the six forms of

[1] The cognitive pattern or Dharmakāya and the operational pattern in its division into being *with* others, Sambhogakāya, and being *in* the world, Nirmāṇakāya.

[2] On this term see note 3, p. 106.

life [1], the demons and evil spirits and others, have been satisfied by the taste of this nectar and that as soon as it permeates us, all emotional upsets together with their latent potentialities become purified by being awakened to enlightenment in the reality of Heruka. We should then experience a strong feeling of joy in thinking that our goal will be achieved because the whole of Saṃsāra becomes empty when we think of the world as a divine realm and thus both the world and the beings in it become transfigured and pure. This whole vision gathers in a brilliant light and dissolves in us. We ourselves dissolve in light which then gathers in the heart-region and becomes translucent like empty space with nothing appearing in it. Then certain of the previously developed unbiased outlook, our mind, radiant in a co-emergent awareness which itself is great bliss, takes no-thing-ness, the existentiality of all that is, as its objective reference. This experience must be taken hold of. When we come out of this composure we should have the implicit faith that this awareness in which bliss and no-thing-ness are individible, being motility and mentation, will rise in the shape of the male-female Heruka, and we should feel intensely proud that we are this co-emergent great bliss-awareness of all Buddhas that thus rises in an operational pattern. Heruka is the symbol for co-emergent bliss-awareness and his spouse, the *yoginī*, is the symbol for existentiality or no-thing-ness [2]. The meaning of the union with the Female in close embrace is that our mind, co-emergent great bliss-awareness, has become of one value with and inseparable from existentiality or no-thing-ness. By being conversant with this symbolism our mind, becoming great bliss, can concentrate on existentiality, no-thing-ness. When we arise out of this state we must think of all that appears as a divine pattern and in addition that it is our mind, the awareness of no-thing-ness in bliss, that rises in this divine shape.

To put it concisely, we must disengage ourselves from wordly affairs by thinking that in this world there is nothing to be relied upon and that we, each for himself, must strive to become able to deliver all beings who are like our aged mother. For this purpose we must develop an enlightened attitude which is the thought that we certainly will reach the citadel of Buddhahood, and then we must develop a middle view and become convinced that our mind is of the nature of great bliss by thinking that

---

[1] Men, gods, demons, animals, spirits, and denizens of hell.

[2] It is important to note that there is no swalling up into an Absolute. The cognitive situation remains relational and intentional in structure.

all appearances are but the projections of our mind and that there is nothing existing in truth [1]. If there is any appearance it will be our mind rising in the shape of Heruka in Male-Female form, and again and again we must think that the whole world and its inhabitants are pure and in a state of transfiguration.

This method, or the essence of the ocean of the Guhyamantra, realized by the saint dbEn-sa-pa and his disciples, is more secret than secret. However, I have written it down in a few words as clearly as possible.

May I ever be watched over until I am enlightened
By the venerable Gurus, gracious beyond compare,
Who embody the Compassion of all Buddhas
And as lords protect us pitiable people.

May I be favoured to expel from my heart the foe,
That veritable ogre, the belief in an 'I',
By whom I have been fooled since time without
Beginning by false promises of wealth.

May I be favoured quickly with deliverance (complete)
From the great ocean of Being, the birth-place of distress,
Of slavery, constant change and the unstable, for I am swept away
By turbulent currents caused by karmic acts and emotional states.

May I be favoured by perfection in supreme
Enlightenment through true compassion when I think
Of the misery and pain in this (great) ocean of Being, of
The beings that are there and are the mother who long sheltered me.

All things within and without like an echo appear
And yet are nothing, they are nothing yet appear.
May I travel this auspicious path quickly to its end, (the path) on which
Appearance and no-thing-ness, fitness of action and intelligence unite.

Good and evil or in whatever way errancy
May appear are but labels that by my mind are used.
May my mind dwell in the sphere of Reality
And not beneath the spell of hope, fear, lust and hate.

To dire illusions may I not succumb,
But may I with heroes and Ḍākas dance
In the circle of the lustrous gods and in the joy
Of the music of co-emergent bliss-no-thing-ness.

---

[1] This is a short recapitulation of the three essentials for setting out on the path of spiritual development: disengagement, goal-consciousness, and unbiased outlook.

May I reach soon the citadel of unity
Where inseparable and in embrace most close
Live the young groom called 'The Great Bliss-Awareness'
And 'Reality' the bride immaculate.

May the Ḍākas of the three realms befriend me (quickly)
So that I write clearly for my own and others' good
This essence of the nectar of instruction
By Vajradhara dbEn-sa-pa Incarnate.

CHAPTER NINE

THE INSTRUCTION IN THE ESSENCE OF THE VAJRAYĀNA PATH OR THE SHORT-CUT TO THE PALACE OF UNITY

At all times I bow to and take refuge in the lotus-feet of my venerable Gurus who are one with Vajradhara.

I pray that they will accept me with compassion.

White moonbeams from the toe-nails of the venerable Gurus
Who relieve us from the fever of our infatuations
When on us falls the light of their compassion,
Have for ever entered the lotus of my heart.

I fold my hands devoutly before Mañjughoṣa
Who fills the sky with his vast benign and wrathful forms,
Who gives the aspirant the Wish-Fulfilling Gem that grants
Boons high and low, thinking of him with love as if his son.

May the host of Ḍākas in the three worlds watch
Over me who fails not in my commitments
Whilst I am guided to the palace of great bliss
Where the treasures of Vajradhara lie concealed.

For a discriminative person who wants to achieve the aim of his next life, because he is not content with merely having a good time now, the single entrance to it is the precious teaching of the Buddha. Since the real gate to this teaching is taking refuge in the Three Jewels [1], intelligent persons first of all will take refuge in them with all their heart. However, it is not enough merely to utter the refuge formula. Above all you have to feel disgusted with the world by thinking how you have been tormented

[1] The Buddha, the Dharma and the Sangha. See note 3, p. 81.

for a long time by the three kinds of misery and have roamed about in this world with its three spheres without any independence because of the power of karmic actions and emotional upsets. Further, thinking that you will suffer this misery uninterruptedly until the emotional tendencies have been eliminated, you must feel frightened and terrified. Lastly, having become absolutely certain by way of clear reasoning that the power to save you from this misery rests with the Three Jewels, you must make your decision and take refuge in them with full confidence.

The graded practice of the path starts after having taken refuge. The compassionate Teacher has proclaimed many ways in view of the disposition and the intellectual acumen of the aspirants, but ultimately they are only a means to become enlightened. As is stated in the *mTshan yang-dag-par brjod-pa:*

> By three ways comes disengagement,
> At the end of one lies rest.

In order to reach the citadel of Buddhahood we must have its causative experience which is the integral unity of fitness of action and intelligence. Otherwise the goal cannot be achieved, as I have shown in my '*Specific Guidance to the Profound Middle View*' [1] where I dealt with that which is common to both the Sūtras and Tantras.

Mahāyāna has been said to consist of the Pāramitāyāna as the cause and Vajrayāna as the climax, and since the latter is the most profound and quickest way to reach the citadel of Buddahood, we must set out with certainty on the Mantrayāna path after we have practised the common way. Tsong-kha-pa has said [2]:

> If perfect Buddhahood you wish to gain
> There are two paths of the profound
> Yānas of Vajra and Pāramitā: but to the last
> The Guhyamantrayāna is far superior: [3]
> This like the sun and moon is known.
> But he who never tries to plumb
> The profundity of this path,
> Just believing it is true,
> Bears the burden of his learning.
> Would it not be shameful for a clever man to leave
> This path unsurpassable, hard for the dull to find?

---

[1] See pp. 104 seqq.

[2] *Tskhp* II 2, 63a.

[3] This is another name for Vajrayāna. See chapter *Pāramitāyāna and Mantrayāna* in part I.

So when I took the oath of the Victorious One,
On the Vajrayāna, more precious than the Buddha,
I strove with all my might to win
The treasures of the two attainments.
It was through you, Mañjughoṣa, priceless gem of knowledge,
That I thought thus and found spiritual satisfaction.

The entrance into the Mantrayāna fold is delineated, according to Tsong-kha-pa [1]:

By practising the common path I have won
Some worth. May I be favoured with an easy
Entrance to the gate through which the fortunate
Set out on the Vajrayāna path supreme.

Thus we have to purify ourselves by means of the common path and acquire a stable feeling of disengagement from worldly affairs, of an enlightened attitude, and of an unbiased outlook. Then we have to cultivate an enlightened attitude and, even if on our part we are indefatigable in working for others until Saṃsāra has become empty, firmly implant the idea in our mind that we are coming nearer the goal whenever we remember that beings are frustrated by misery. In so doing we set out on the Vajrayāna path, the profound short-cut that brings us quickly to the citadel of Buddhahood.

The Mantrayāna method is quicker and more profound than the Pāramitāyāna because it provides for the special instruction by which the goal itself is made the path, a procedure and technique not found in the Pāramitāyāna. Further, in the Mantrayāna it is the Anuttarayogatantra that has the power to make us realize the dual pattern of existence in a single mental act by meditating on no-thing-ness, and in particular it is a short-cut because it produces the special awareness so necessary for overcoming that straying of the mind which becomes the belief in things as existing in truth.

The method of making the goal the path is as follows: You have to purify and transfigure whatever appears as the world and its beings, within which you ordinarily become involved by your appetance, by thinking of them as a pure environment and its inhabitants. That is to say, no longer preoccupied with your physical aspect you think of it as being Vajrasattva [2] and the same with your environment until it becomes

---

[1] *Tskhp* II 2, 3a.
[2] See note 2, p. 100.

transfigured into a realm of purity. Similarly your communications become sacred vessels of worship, manifesting themselves in their true nature, and your actions assume the character of Buddha-activities. The Mantrayāna path in general and the Anuttarayogatantra path in particular are quick ways because, by thinking of unlimited purities in the manner detailed above, your two piles of knowlegde and merits approach perfection more and more every moment. You then become capable of quickly removing the heavy stains of your karmic actions; you develop the power of having the favour of the Buddhas and their spiritual sons always present. In the Anuttarayogatantra path, in addition, there is a special co-emergent awareness on the subjective side, through the power of which the latent disposition of the mind to stray into the belief in things as existing in truth is quickly overcome. On the objective side, however, it is not different from the other paths, taking no-thingness or the existentiality of all that is as its objective reference. Thus by a single mental process the operational patterns [1] as well as the cognitive one [2] are simultaneously realized.

This Vajrasattvayoga, effecting a complete fourfold purity [3] and uniting fitness of action with intelligence in an indivisible manner, is also called Vajrayāna, Phalayāna, and Guhyamantrayāna.

---

[1] These are in the technical language of the Tantras the Sambhogakāya representing the communicative norm, the being *with* others, and the Nirmāṇakāya or the being *in* the world. See also note 1, p. 95.

[2] Dharmakāya.

[3] Vajrasattvayoga may be translated in view of the meaning of Vajrasattva as elucitaded in note 2, p. 95, as 'an attempt to live up to man's existential norms'. The analysis of the humain individual, which is particularly penetrating in Buddhist Tantrism, shows that man is not a selfenclosed substance with certain relations incidentally attached to it. Man's whole being is intentional in structure and how he orders his life and the world he lives in depends on his becoming aware (or remaining unaware) of these norms which are not determinate traits or properties but ways of being that are active and dynamic. The better these norms are understood the better is man's relation to others and the more significant are his actions. Thus sound insight into the nature of man and action in the light of his knowledge reinforce each other. The same is true of their opposites. In the religious-symbolic language of the Tantras this means that when we become aware of our existential norms the drabness of our ordinary life, which may be said to be an absence from one's norms, is transfigured. These four 'purities' then are: (I) the world we live in and which so often we are accustomed to decry as a vale of tears, becomes a Buddha-realm of infinite beauty; (II) man himself instead of being looked at and dealt with as a thing, becomes a subject, a 'god' (which is by no means a deification of man, for such deification is but a confusion of the divine

Among the Vajrayāna Tantras there are the Kriyā-, Caryā-, Yoga-, and Anuttarayoga-tantras [1]. The best among them, since it shows the short-cut which leads to the citadel of Buddhahood in a single short lifetime during this evil age, is the Anuttarayogatantra.

Tsong-kha-pa tells us how to set out on it [2]:

When by practising the common path you are a worthy vessel,
Then the four initiations will empower you to practise
The Two Stages which abolish the four kinds of impurity
And impart the (needed) power to live up to the four norms [3].

From a competent Guru you have to obtain the four initiatory empowerments and whilst receiving them you have to guard your commitments [4] and restraints [5] like the apple of your eye. In particular it has been said that it is very difficult for virtue to grow in us when we are polluted by not keeping our commitments and that therefore we should stake our life on not becoming defiled by violating them. If, on the other hand, the commitments and restraints are kept firmly we will certainly attain enlightenment in less than sixteen re-in-carnations. In our earnest striving we have to make the observation of our commitments and restraints the basis of all our endeavour. By discarding them our efforts, however great they may be, will all come to nought. It would be like expecting fruits to grow on a tree that has been cut at the root. All saintly sages say the same.

After we have made the commitments and restraints our foundation we then must set out on the path of the Two Stages [6]. We must practise

---

with the human. In the end it serves merely as a means to despise all others and to insist on their thingness); (III) whatever one possesses or uses becomes the vehicle of worship; and (IV) whatever one does is authentic action, not an escape from ones obligations.

[1] These four kinds of Tantras each deal with certain developmental aspects as the proceed from an 'outer' form of ritual acts and ways of acting to an 'inner' form of pure philosophy as a means of organizing one's whole life.

[2] *Tskph* II 2, 274b.

[3] The four norms are Nirmāṇakāya, Sambhogakāya, Dharmakāya, and Svābhāvikakāya. As to their meaning see note 1 p. 95, and notes 2 and 3, p. 97. Each initiatory empowerment relates to one of these norms and aims at removing those obstacles which prevent the individual from living up to his norms.

[4] There are nineteen commitments which are distributed over the five 'Buddha-families' or *leitmotifs*, value and action patterns.

[5] There are two kinds, those of a Bodhisattva in general and the fourteen restraints incumbent on every follower of the Tantric discipline. As to the latter see note 1, pp. 99 seqq.

[6] Developing Stage and Fulfilment Stage.

them by having learned them from true spiritual friends who are well versed in the matter and whom we have served properly. In the beginning, we have to attend to the Developing Stage and have a vivid experience of it. Afterwards we can practise the Fulfilment Stage. Tsong-kha-pa has declared that without having the experience of the Developing Stage, the Fulfilment Stage will not be realized, even if we attempt to practise it. In order to create a disposition for it it is of the utmost importance again and again to attempt the Two Stages.

When at the phase of the Developing Stage we have become mentally conversant with the means of transmuting birth, death and the intermediate state into the three Buddha norms [1], we must master completely the elements of the realization techniques which competent saints and sages have explained as the intention of the Yogatantra. Within the circle of a *maṇḍala* complete in every respect, we have to feel the divine pride and have a clear vision of the deity. Through having a strong interest in this process, thereby experiencing vividly the non-duality of clarity and profoundness, many stains of karmic actions are wiped clean and countless merits accumulated. Further, by first practising the Developing Stage it becomes a special power for maturing all that is necessary for the profound Fulfilment Stage, so that the latter is easily attained and develops perfectly. While starting with the practice of the Fulfilment Stage, after we have mastered the Developing Stage, it is of the greatest importance to know how to immerse ourselves in our existentiality by illumining the three structural ways [2] with their four focal points [3] when

---

[1] Death is related to the Dharmakāya, the intermediate state to the Sambhogakāya, and birth to the Nirmāṇakāya. See above pp. 101 seq. where the meditational experiences have been described. Death, intermediate state and birth have a figurative meaning in this context, not a physical one.

[2] The complex of the three *rtsa* (*nāḍi*). This diagram of the body's anatomy must not be considered as an attempt to describe real anatomical conditions. Every attempt to do so has failed and was bound to fail, because the purpose of this diagram is of a different nature. When vividly imagined and mentally incorporated it lends itself admirably to a severance of the ties of assumption about the body. The three path-ways, a central one with two others to the right and left of it, not only relate to the body as such but also to the mental processes as a polarization between the 'I' as knower and the thing known.

[3] The four focal points are 'situated' in the head, the throat, the heart and the navel. However, since the meditational diagram of the body has nothing to do with the anatomical one we find in scientific works on anatomy, there actually is no 'situation' as such. They may be considered as focal points of experience related to existential norms.

making the Guruyoga [1] the way to it. Although the various Tantras and the saintly sages in their instructions have described this technique differently they all agree that the concentration center is in the heart focal point, of which Ghaṇṭapāda spoke from the beginning. It has been said that all understanding in the Fulfilment Stage must stem from immersion in one's existentiality, which must take place mainly in the heart focal point. This is because the essential feature of the Fulfilment Stage, the realization of both the apparitional existence and the radiant light (the fact of no-thing-ness and its cognition), depends on unravelling the 'knots' in the heart.

The Fulfilment Stage, which has come about from this immersion in one's existentiality, comprises five steps. Through the experience of this fivefold process one reaches the goal or unity which is the citadel of Vajradhara.

While this goal unity need not be studied further since the pure act of existing (the apparitional being) and the pure noetic power (the real radiancy) have found their ultimate unity, the causes for realizing the operational norms [2] in the act of existing and for the realization of the cognitive norm [3] are an awareness in which bliss unites indivisibly with no-thing-ness. To attain these operational norms the follower of the Pāramitāyāna must accumulate merits for three 'countless aeons'. In the case of a follower of the Anuttarayogatantra it is the power of this apparitional being that perfects the accumulation of merits in a single lifetime. Further, a follower of the Pāramitāyāna must gather knowledge for many 'countless aeons' in order to disperse his intellectual fog, while a follower of the Anuttarayogatantra achieves this by the power of his awareness in which bliss is indivisible from no-thing-ness. Because of this double power the Anuttarayogatantra path is a very quick one. Inasmuch as the realization of an apparitional being depends on the awareness in which bliss unites indivisibly with no-thing-ness, this awareness is the core of the path and the ultimate short-cut to becoming enlightened in a single short lifetime during this evil age. Even so, since certainty about the ultimate nature of this bliss and no-thing-ness is very rare, few have travelled the path to its end, although many believe in it, and those few are like a star in the noon sky.

---

[1] This is a meditational technique which varies according to the succession of the Gurus with the different schools.

[2] Rūpakāya, See note 3, p. 105.

[3] Dharmakāya, *Ibid*, note 5.

What is this ultimate bliss and no-thing-ness [1]? Well, how can a simpleton like me know discursively what is a thoroughly mystic experience? When I discussed that which is common to the Sūtras and Tantras I stated the ultimate nature of the profound or no-thing-ness in a manner easy to understand, according to that which I have learned from my Gurus. But this great bliss, the subjective factor, is more secret than the secret and more subtle than the subtle, to say nothing of how it develops in us. Even as an object of thought it is most difficult to understand.

When through full concentration the mind has become stable, it has a feeling tone of relaxed contentment. The moment this has been achieved, the vibrations permeating the body from head to heel become supple and the body feels pleasantly at ease. Due to this there is an intense feeling of bodily pleasure and mental delight. But such pleasure and delight are nothing in comparison with that which has been termed 'co-emergent great bliss' in the Anuttarayogatantras. This concentration involving bodily ease and mental delight is common to both outsiders and insiders; the former use it to feel on top of the world, the latter to scale the higher spiritual levels within the three courses. In this way such a concentration with its feeling of ease and delight is a common feature of the worldly and transworldly paths. The fact, however, that the co-emergent great bliss has been derived from immersion in one's existentiality when one practises the Fulfilment Stage (following one's mastery of the Developing Stage on the highest Mantrayāna path which, in turn, is based on the completion of the journey along the common path) marks this as being a very high way within the Mantrayāna. Hence it is as different from the previously mentioned ordinary concentration as are heaven and earth. Although it has been said that intense ease and delight are felt when one practises breath-control as detailed in the *Śrāvakabhūmi* [2] and the *Abhidharma* [3], or when one concentrates on the deity of one's choice by gathering the vibrations within instead of letting them become dispersed into the without as described in the *Dhyānottarapaṭalakrama* and the *Vairocanābhisambodhitantra* and other Kriyā- and Caryātantras, this also is as nothing in comparison with the co-emergent bliss of the Anuttarayogatantras. The reason is that however deep the

---

[1] A more elaborate account is given in Ye-shes rgyal-mtshan's *Lam-gyi dka'-gnas-la dogs-pa gcod-tshul zab-don snang-ba*, foll, 13a seq. There he follows closely *Tskhp* VII 1, 52b seq.

[2] This is one of the five divisions of the *Yogācārabhūmi.*

[3] The *Abhidharmasamuccaya* by Asanga.

understanding of the Pāramitāyāna and of the three lower Tantras [1] may be, there is not a single instruction in them about the practice of the Two Stages, the commitments and restraints and the initiatory empowerments making a person suited for experiencing the sublime Fulfilment Stage spoken of in the Anuttarayogatantras. Therefore, the difference between the concentration with its special feeling of ease and delight as explained in the Pāramitāyāna and the three lower Tantras, and the concentration with the co-emergent bliss feeling as spoken of in the Anuttarayogatantras, is as big as that between the sky and the palm of your hand. This is still not the last word. It has been stated that when after long practice we directly and without internal warping intuit the existentiality of all that is, no-thing-ness, a most marvelous feeling of serene happiness is born. Above that, when one reaches the first spiritual level 'The Joyful One' of the Mahāyanist path of seeing [2] even this serene happiness is not the co-emergent bliss of the Anuttarayogatantras. It may be pointed out that this first spiritual level is called the Joyful One because on it a most marvelous feeling of ease and delight is felt.

In this connection it has been said that even the. Buddha-sons, who have become masters of the ten spiritual levels by having travelled the Pāramitāyāna path through accumulating knowledge and merits during many 'countless aeons', when they finally approach enlightenment, must enter the Anuttarayoga path, receive instructions from a competent Guru and realize this co-emergent great bliss. Therefore the moment we learn of this unique short-cut to the citadel of Buddhahood in this brief life and evil age, we have to prepare the ground by thinking of this short-cut of which it is difficult to hear in countless aeons.

What, then, is its secret? It has been said that by immersing ourselves in our existentiality the outward projections of the motor activities cease and all vibrations move towards, continue, and dissolve in the central path of the existential structure. Because of this the 'fire' in the navel and sex regions is kindled and the *HAṂ* in the head region begins to melt [3]. In connection with this there arises a wondrous feeling of happiness

---

[1] The Kriyā-, Caryā- and Yogatantras.

[2] See note 2, p. 92.

[3] This symbolism relates to a process which may be said to be an attempt to harmonize and bring about an integral unity of vitality and mentality. The former is symbolized by the letter *A* and likened to fire, the latter by the *HAṂ* which, by the fire of the former, is made to leave its isolation and frozenness. Our own language suggests something similar by speaking of 'warmer' feelings and of 'cold'

which is proportionate to and simultaneous with the feeling of the mind being gradually emptied of its contents when the mind-moving forces cease to operate.

What is the meaning of uniting bliss with no-thing-ness in an indivisible manner? It does not mean to bring bliss and its no-thing-ness together. Since any thing is the indivisibility of its no-thing-ness and factuality ever since being this or that thing, the *yogi* need not bring the two together. If bliss and no-thing-ness are separate entities from the beginning, the *yogi* will never be able to unite them indivisibly; and if they are indivisible from the beginning, the *yogi* can never separate them, however much he may try. In view of this fact the *Prajñāpāramitāsūtras* many times have asserted:

> Not as two existing and not to be divided into two.

Neither does it mean to seal bliss with no-thing-ness and *vice versa*. The statement that the good of liberality and other virtues is to be 'sealed with seeing', means that in order to quiet the tendency to believe in the goodness of an action we have to investigate its nature and see that it is not something with a being of its own. But this does not lead to the indivisibility of bliss and no-thing-ness.

Nor does it mean to make an affectation of seeing. This happens when someone starts a certain mood and out of this affected feeling that everything is of an apparitional nature distributes gifts, observes ethics and manners and engages in other activities. Now, liberality is a readiness to give; to see no-thing-ness is the cognition that all things do not exist by virtue of a principle through which they are what they are. In no way does the readiness to give become the seeing of no-thing-ness.

Lastly, first to develop a point of view and then seal it with bliss would split the mind into a previous and subsequent part and there is no reason why the two parts should become single and indivisible. Therefore the great Saraha has said:

> They talk of it in every house,
> Yet they know not where the great bliss dwells.

---

reason. Together the two letters form *AHAM* which is the Sanskrit word for 'I'. Ordinarily there is a split between feelings and thoughts. Their unity forms the 'I', but this does not mean that now a new 'I' is brought into the picture after one has taken all the trouble to show that there is no 'I' existing as such. These symbols are merely operational counters. In going along a way or a path man must have an idea of where he is going and he traverses the path in the light of his projects. On this interpretation of the 'I' see also *Tskhp* VI 3, 23b seq.

Thus, when such knowledge is already very rare, what are we to say of the way this co-emergent great bliss and no-thing-ness grow in us? A proper understanding seems to be something very exceptional.

What, then, is to be understood by the union of bliss with no-thing-ness? Although simpletons like me cannot say that it is ultimately this or that, yet according to bLo-bzang rdo-rje-'chang chen-po [1] it is like this. When we practise that which happens when the great bliss makes the ultimate no-thing-ness its objective constituent, we achieve that which is meant by uniting bliss with no-thing-ness in an indivisible manner. To give an example: When we speak of practising faith we mean that our mind becomes of the nature of faith. Similarly, to unite bliss with no-thing-ness means that our mind which is this great bliss becomes a mind which understands no-thing-ness [2]. This is also said to be like pouring water into water.

Thus, in order to reach the citadel of Vajradhara, the goal unity, a study of this unity must precede its realization; and in order to reach this goal the experience of the real radiant light must be had earlier. Before this there must be the realization of apparitional existence, before this the semblance light [3] or the union of bliss with no-thing-ness by immersing ourselves in our existentiality, before this the practice of the coarse and subtle forms of the Developing Stage, before this the initiatory empowerments and the proper observation of all commitments and restraints, before this the purification of ourselves by traversing the common path, and before this the service of spiritual friends as the source of the acquisition of all that is positive.

---

[1] Tsong-kha-pa as one with Vajradhara.

[2] We must be careful not to misread this statement and rashly judge that here an identification with the Absolute is propounded. The Buddhists, unlike many other philosophers in the East and West, have distinguished clearly between a 'formal' identification and an 'existential' one. The noetic act, 'great bliss' as it is symbolically termed, is there as an indeterminate relational form which becomes terminated by the object, no-thing-ness. A peculiar type of relational union is achieved where formal identity is involved. This analysis is strikingly similar to the one given by John Wild, *The Challenge of Existentialism*, Bloomington. Indiana University Press, 1955, p. 226.

[3] The distinction between the 'real light' and the 'semblance light' refers to the phases of the path and the goal-attainment. Just as practising the existential norms such as Nirmāṇakāya and so on, is not these norms themselves, so also the luminous experiences are not the light itself, and hence are termed 'semblance light'.

This condensation of all the essential features of both the Sūtras and Tantras into a single path, beginning with the service of spiritual friends and ending with the attainment of integral unity, is the unfailing means to win enlightenment in this short life of ours in an evil age by a man who is like a precious jewel [1]. This is what my Gurus have told me.

May I ever be watched over by Mañjughoṣa who can cross the ocean of the Tantras swelled by Kriyā-, Caryā-,
Yoga- and Anuttara-yoga, the four great Tantric rivers that flow down from the snow mountain of non-dual teaching,
Enriched by treasures of instruction, commitment and restraint, while the Two Stages rest upon the earth of the gem-like mind,
They are most hard to fathom because they are stirred up by many words, the six confines [2] and the four ways of explanation [3].

I have elucidated and not been fanciful
About the nectar flowing from the lotus-mouth
Of all-knowing Tsong-kha-pa in the accustomed manner

---

[1] The Vajrayāna path is open to the 'superior individual' who has traversed the common path and by having had the experience of that which is involved with the lower stages of the inferior and mediocre individuals, has built himself a solid foundation. Buddhism has always been aware of the intellectual differences and capacities of human individuals, because it addresses itself to the concrete man and not to an abstraction. So also among the superior individuals different people are to be found. There are five types of them which are known by the designations of 'blue lotus', 'white lotus', 'red lotus', 'sandal wood', and 'precious jewel'. This classification which is found in Candrakīrti's commentary on the *Guhysamājatantra*, the *Pradīpoddyotana-nāma-ṭikā*, has been commented upon by Tsong-kha-pa in *Tskhp* IV 13ab as follows: A man who understands the meaning whilst studying, but easily forgets what he has learned, is like a 'blue lotus', because as long as it stays in the water it is extremely fragrant, but as soon as it is taken out of the water it fades and loses its fragrance. A man who is learned but fails to transmit his knowledge is like a 'white lotus', because this flower keeps its fragrance within its centre and does not disperse it. A man whose mind opens when he studies but with whom knowledge does not last long, is like a 'red lotus' which opens when the sun rises but soon after loses the dew-drops resting on it. A man who is very proud of his learning even if it does not amount to much and brags a lot, is like 'sandal wood', because the sandal wood tree beaιs no fruit, has but little fragrance and is full of thorns. A man, however, who strictly observes that to which he has committed himself and studies deeply so as to transmit his knowledge to others, is like a 'precious jewel', difficult to find.

[2] The six confines of discourse are: the direct meaning, the suggestive meaning, the actual intention of the Buddha's words, that which is not the actual intention, the exact words of the Buddha's, and that which is not the exact words.

[3] The four ways are: the word for word explanation, the genereal meaning, the hidden meaning, and the ultimate meaning.

Of the Gurus of the spiritual tradition.
Since the Anuttarayoga has no room
For simpletons like me infatuated,
If I have stated something wrong or betrayed a secret
Too plainly, I confess my sin to Vajradhara.
May all beings who suffer like my mother
By the nectar of great bliss be satisfied
Through any good I may have written
Due to the favour of my Gurus.
From the friends that I have made on this path supreme
I will never separate in the times to come.
Soon will I reach the citadel of Him who has ten powers [1], for I
Will realize and tread the path auspicious on which one may not err.

---

[1] See note 4, p. 104.

INDEX